LET'S LEARN ABOUT...
THE OCEAN

Teacher's Guide
Pre-coding

K1

P Pearson

Pearson Education Limited
KAO Two, KAO Park, Harlow, Essex, CM17 9NA, England
and Associated Companies around the world.

© Pearson Education Limited 2020

The right of Luciana Pinheiro and Rhiannon Ball, to be identified as authors of this Work has been asserted by them in accordance with the Copyright, Designs and Patents Act 1988.

All rights reserved; no part of this publication may be reproduced, stored in a retrieval system, or transmitted in any form or by any means, electronic, mechanical, photocopying, recording, or otherwise without the prior written permission of the Publishers.

First published 2020

ISBN: 978-1-292-33408-0

Set in Mundo Sans
Printed in China (SWTC/01)

Acknowledgements
The publishers and author(s) would like to thank the following people and institutions for their feedback and comments during the development of the material: Marcos Mendonça, Leandra Dias, Viviane Kirmeliene, Rhiannon Ball, Simara H. Dal'Alba, Mônica Bicalho and GB Editorial. The publishers would also like to thank all the teachers who contributed to the development of *Let's learn about...*: Adriano de Paula Souza, Aline Ramos Teixeira Santo, Aline Vitor Rodrigues Pina Pereira, Ana Paula Gomez Montero, Anna Flávia Feitosa Passos, Camila Jarola, Celiane Junker Silva, Edegar França Junior, Fabiana Reis Yoshio, Fernanda de Souza Thomaz, Luana da Silva, Michael Iacovino Luidvinavicius, Munique Dias de Melo, Priscila Rossatti Duval Ferreira Neves, Sandra Ferito, and schools that took part in Construindo Juntos.

Author Acknowledgements
Luciana Pinheiro, Rhiannon Ball

Illustration Acknowledgements
Illustrated by Filipe Laurentino and Silva Serviços de Educação.

Cover illustration © Filipe Laurentino

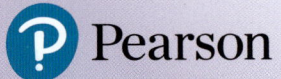

Contents

	Table of contents	4
	Presentation	6
U1	How are we all similar?	8
U2	How are we all different?	12
U3	What is a family?	16
U4	Do you share your toys?	20
U5	How do you help at home?	24
U6	How do you take care of your pet?	28
U7	What is your favorite food?	32
U8	What do you like about school?	36

Table of contents – Pre-coding

UNIT	LESSON 1	LESSON 2
Unit 1 How are we all similar? page 8	• Color shapes in a sequence • Recognize and use words for shapes and colors **Pre-coding skill:** • Sequence	• Make an algorithm for a song • Identify and practice using words for parts of the body and face **Pre-coding skill:** • Algorithm
Unit 2 How are we all different? page 12	• Complete a symmetrical drawing • Identify and name parts of the face **Pre-coding skill:** • Symmetry	• Teach and do a repeated sequence of actions • Recognize and use words for numbers and body parts **Pre-coding skill:** • Looping
Unit 3 What is a family? page 16	• Identify an incorrect element (a "bug") in a sequence • Count to five **Pre-coding skill:** • Debugging	• Recognize and complete a pattern • Identify and practice using words for family members **Pre-coding skill:** • Pattern
Unit 4 Do you share your toys? page 20	• Create a symmetrical pattern • Practice using words for toys **Pre-coding skill:** • Symmetry	• Match conditions to results • Identify and follow commands **Pre-coding skill:** • Branching (*If-Then*)

UNIT	LESSON 1	LESSON 2
Unit 5 How do you help at home? page 24	• Identify and follow a sequence • Talk about helping at home **Pre-coding skill:** • Sequence	• Break down a large number into smaller ones • Identify and practice saying numbers up to nine **Pre-coding skill:** • Decomposition
Unit 6 How do you take care of your pet? page 28	• Match conditions to results • Practice talking about pets and how to take care of them **Pre-coding skill:** • Branching (If-Then)	• Identify an incorrect element (a "bug") in a sequence • Identify and name animals **Pre-coding skill:** • Debugging
Unit 7 What is your favorite food? page 32	• Make an algorithm for a song • Practice using words for food **Pre-coding skill:** • Sequence	• Identify and follow a sequence • Identify and name fruits **Pre-coding skill:** • Sequence
Unit 8 What do you like about school? page 36	• Make an algorithm • Ask and answer about locations **Pre-coding skill:** • Programming	• Identify and complete a pattern • Identify and use words for classroom objects **Pre-coding skill:** • Pattern

Presentation

Let's learn about... is a bilingual program which aims to develop a wide variety of skills and knowledge of different subjects. To this end, several additional components ensure that students work on creative learning, pre-coding, STEAM lessons, personal, social, and emotional development, and much more. Teachers can find a complete mapping of the components online and suggested weekly planning to help them make the most of the interdisciplinary approach. All of the components in the program provide students with the opportunity to build a solid foundation and prepare themselves for the challenges ahead. The lessons help children explore and learn more about the world around them. The Pre-coding Project Book helps students explore and learn more about the digital world around them.

What is coding?

Coding is a programming language that is used to get a computer to behave how you want it to. It is present in everyday life, in all of the machines and technology that we use on a daily basis. Think about when you wash clothes: how does a modern washing machine know when to start? When you press "go" on the digital screen, a pre-programmed code tells the washing machine that it needs to start the wash cycle.

Learning principles behind Pre-coding in *Let's learn about...*

Children of preschool and kindergarten age in the 21st Century are living in a rapidly changing world that is dominated by continuously evolving technology. These children are digital natives, which means that they don't know a life without smartphones, the Internet, computers, etc. Most will be used to handling and playing with technology, so they are already ready to start working on something that can be challenging and even intimidating for many adults: coding.

Computer programmers need to have well-developed problem-solving, logical thinking, and decision-making skills to program codes and find problems in codes when a computer isn't behaving the way it should. Therefore, the Pre-coding component in ***Let's learn about...*** aims to help students develop these important skills. We want students to start thinking like computer programmers, and this is best done through play. That's why the Pre-coding component is completely screenless.

Students will start developing skills through fun games, drawing, coloring and sticker activities, and hands-on activities, working both individually and with their classmates. All of these activities lay an important foundation for students to start coding with real computers when they move on in their learning journey.

What's in a Pre-coding lesson?

Pre-coding lessons follow similar routines to the ones that students develop in all the ***Let's learn about...*** components, including the visual schedule, attention-getters, and *hello* and *goodbye* songs and routines.

Each lesson works on a coding skill, with students taking part in a teacher-led activity before putting this into practice through a hands-on activity in the Project Book. Lessons are topic-based according to the core Student's Book, so students have the opportunity to practice their language skills further.

Although the concept is screen-free, you may like to spark students' interest and imagination by telling them that they are computer programmers in these classes, and their job is to make things happen and fix problems, just like real computer programmers! A fun computer character appears occasionally throughout the Project Book to reinforce this activity and to add a level of familiarity, which is important for students of this age.

Pre-coding Glossary

The Pre-coding component works on the following coding skills and concepts. These are explained throughout the Teacher's Guide. From K2 onwards, you may like to start using these words with your students, but avoid giving long, complex explanations or expecting them to understand the meaning. Simply use the word as you are demonstrating or participating in an activity.

Algorithm: Refers to a sequence of instructions that tells a computer to do something.
Decomposition: Refers to breaking down a problem into smaller parts that are easier to deal with.
Debugging: Refers to identifying mistakes in a code (or pattern). In coding, mistakes in patterns are called "bugs" and they stop the computer doing what it should do.
If-Then: Refers to a concept of action and consequence, e.g. *if* this is true, *then* this will happen/is true. In coding, computers make choices depending on whether something is true or not. In this activity, students jump to the correct side of the rope according to if it's correct or not.
Looping: Refers to an algorithm (set of instructions) that repeats a certain number until a specific result is achieved.
Pattern: When there is a problem with a program or app the coders look for patterns that they have not seen before. If they find these patterns, they will know what is wrong and they will be able to fix it.
Symmetry: Refers to a shape looking exactly the same as another one when you move it in the same way.
Sequencing: Refers to organizing objects, numbers, etc. in a specific order. In coding, sequences tell the computer the order in which they need to do things.
Variables: Refers to where information is stored, and it is a factor that can change.

Components

For teachers
- Pre-coding Teacher's Guide
- Audio library with songs available at Pearson English Portal

For students
- Pre-coding Project Book with stickers

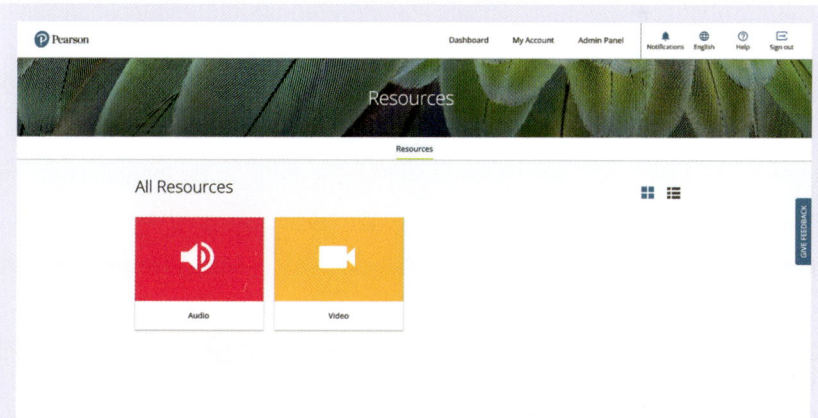

Presentation 7

Unit 1 How are we all similar?

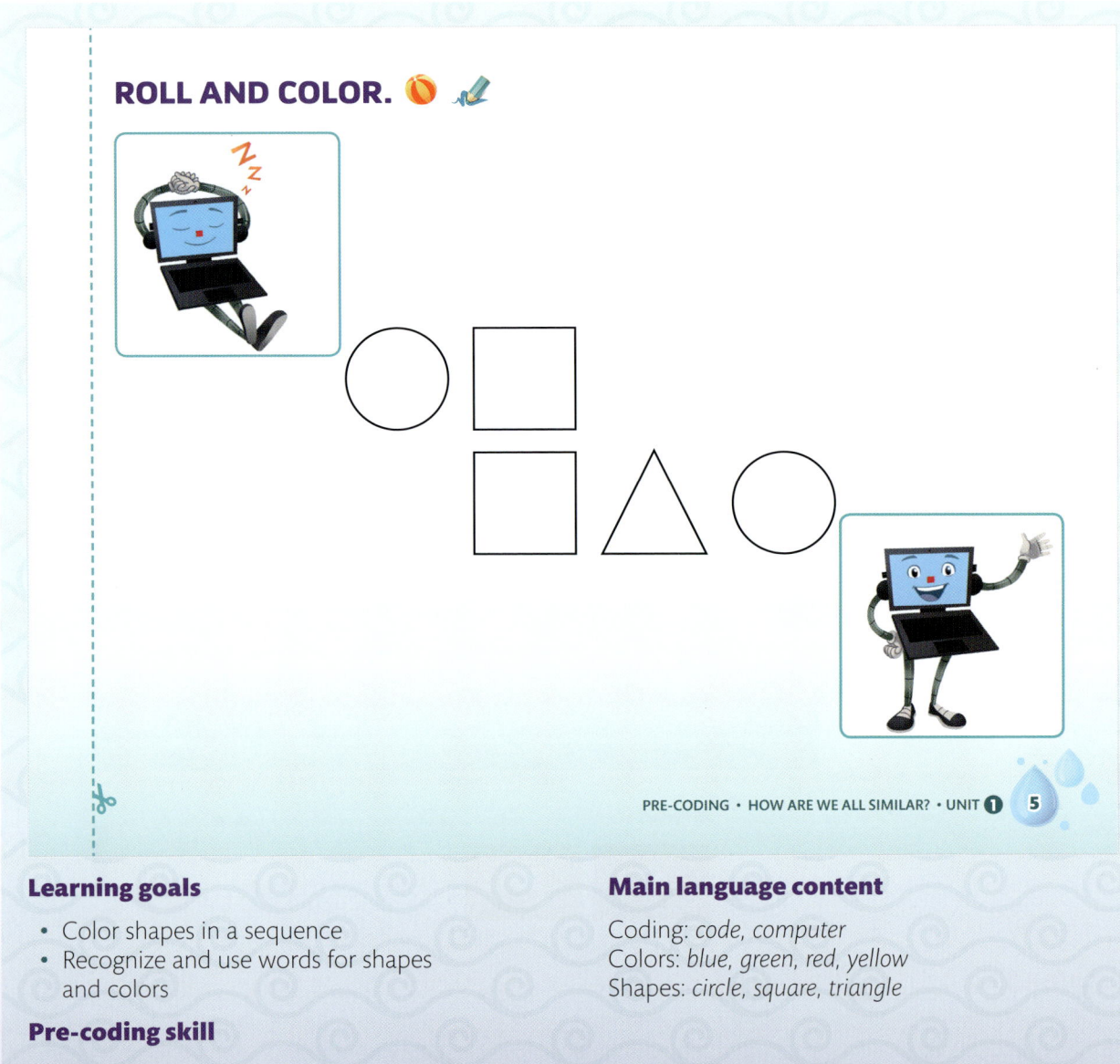

OPENING

Circle time
Materials and preparation
- Audio library – songs
- Puppet

Say *hello* to students and encourage them to greet you back. Introduce the puppet to those who haven't met it or ask for students' help to do so.
Sing the *Hello song* (track 04) and have them sing, mime, and dance. Have students sit in a circle. Choose a name for the puppet together with the class if this hasn't already been done in another class.
Teach students the opening attention-getter:
T: *Let's take this road!*
S: *It's time to code!*
or
T: *Turn on your fun mode because it's time to…*
S: *Code!*
Explain to students that whenever you use an attention-getter, they should stop talking and look at you.

> **Note to teachers**
> You can also teach/review the attention-getter *All set? You bet!*

What's the schedule for today's lesson?
Materials and preparation
- Visual schedule pictures

Show each picture and then separate the ones that show the activities of today's class. Have a volunteer place the pictures of the activities in the middle of the circle.

> **Note to teachers**
> Although students won't be using screens during these activities, a "computer" character will appear to help them associate the basic function of coding, which is to get a computer to achieve a specific task. They will develop pre-coding skills in all lessons; however, in lessons with the computer character, you can be

Learning goals
- Color shapes in a sequence
- Recognize and use words for shapes and colors

Pre-coding skill
- Sequence

Main language content
Coding: *code, computer*
Colors: *blue, green, red, yellow*
Shapes: *circle, square, triangle*

more explicit in explaining that they are "coders" and they need to help the computer do something.

ACTIVE LEARNING

Color jump

Materials and preparation

- Flashcards: *blue, green, red, yellow; circle, square, triangle* (a copy of a flashcard per student)

Show the flashcards one-by-one and review the colors and shapes with students. Ask them to stand up. Give each student a copy of a flashcard. Mime jumping and say *jump*. Encourage students to join in until they understand. Call out the colors and shapes randomly – students holding that flashcard have to jump up and down. Have students switch flashcards and continue the activity for some time.

Color die

Materials and preparation

- Crayons: blue, green, red, and yellow
- Die cutout (available in the Teacher's Resources; a copy per student, pre-cut)
- Several blocks – blue, green, red, and yellow – in a bag (optional)

Give each student a die cutout. They should color four sides of the die using the crayons. In one blank space, draw an X, and in the other blank space, write the student's name. Help them fold and stick the cutout to make the die. You may like to teach the word "die" and allow them to practice rolling it.

If you don't have much time, you can use several blocks of these colors in a bag. Have students take one of the blocks of the bag and name the color. Then in the following activity, they use it to color the shapes on page 5 of the Project Book.

Note to teachers

Coding involves a computer following a specific order, or "sequencing". Learning to order objects in a specific sequence is a basic skill to help students transition to coding later on.

Roll and color.

Materials and preparation

- Crayons: blue, green, red, and yellow
- Project Book page 5
- Several blocks (blue, green, red, and yellow) in a bag (optional)
- Students' color dice

Help students open their Project Book to page 5. If necessary, review the shapes. Point to the picture of the computer on the left and encourage students to tell you that it is sleeping. Ask them to find the "awake" computer. Explain that they are going to be "coders" to help the computer wake up. Ask a volunteer student to come to the front with their die and roll it. The student says the color that the die lands on. Ask the other students to color the first shape in their book in that color. Repeat this step with two other students. For the final two shapes, ask students to roll their own dice and color the shapes.

If you don't have much time, you can use the blocks in the bag. Have students take one of the blocks of the bag, name the color and color the first shape the same color. Repeat the procedure until they have colored all the shapes.

Wake up, computer!

Materials and preparation

- Flashcards: *blue, green, red, yellow; circle, square, triangle*
- Project Book page 5

Divide the class into two groups and have them sit opposite each other. Give one group the shapes flashcards and the other group the colors flashcards. Then ask a volunteer student to be the "sleeping" computer and stand at one end of the open space between the two groups. Another volunteer can be the "awake" computer and stands at the other end. Invite a volunteer student to stand up with their Project Book. That student calls out the code in their book, e.g. *blue circle*. Monitor and help as needed. One student from each group brings the corresponding flashcard and places it in front of the "sleeping computer". When the "code" is complete, the student runs along the flashcards to the "awake" computer and pretends to wake them up.

You should set up expectations of walking safely so as to avoid accidents.

Note to teachers

Collect students' dice at the end of the activity, so that you can keep them to be reused in future activities.

DIFFERENTIATED INSTRUCTION

BELOW LEVEL
Roll and color.

Put all below-level students in a group and do the rolling and coloring as a whole group, or pair up below- and above-level students to roll their dice together.

ABOVE LEVEL
Roll and color.

Students can roll their own dice to color all of the shapes.

CLOSING

Play *Pass the ball*. Sing the *Goodbye song*.

Materials and preparation

- A ball
- Audio library – songs
- Flashcards: *blue, green, red, yellow*

Have students stand up and make a circle. Put the color flashcards in the middle of the circle. Students pass a ball around as they sing the *Goodbye song* (track 05). When you pause the song, call out a color. The student with the ball takes the flashcard from the middle of the circle and repeats the color.

Note to teachers

If necessary, allow the other students to help their classmate identify the correct flashcard.

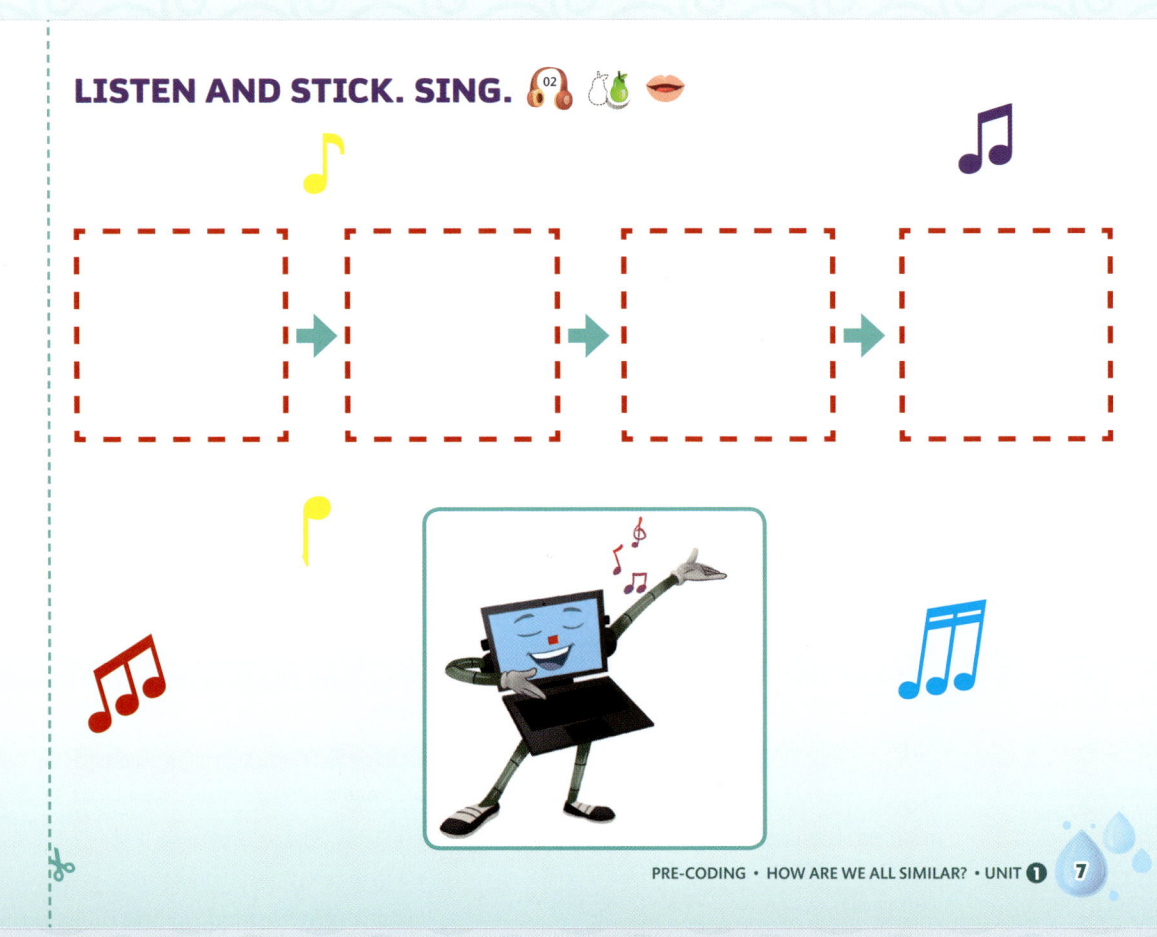

Learning goals
- Make an algorithm for a song
- Identify and practice using words for parts of the body and face

Pre-coding skill
- Algorithm

Main language content

Touch your (nose).
Parts of the face: ears, eyes, mouth, nose

OPENING

Circle time

Materials and preparation
- Puppet
- Visual schedule pictures

Show the puppet to students and have them greet it with *hello* or *hi*. Remind students of the attention-getter and practice it with them:
T: *Let's take this road!*
S: *It's time to code!*
or
T: *Turn on your fun mode because it's time to…*
S: *Code!*
Show students the visual schedule pictures. Ask for volunteers to help you turn them over. Encourage the whole class to say what each picture shows. Ask students to help you select the pictures that show today's schedule as you tell them what they are going to do today.

> **Note to teachers**
> Remind students that they should be quiet and pay attention when you use the attention-getter.

Touch your nose!

Have students sit in a circle. Point to the parts of your face (*ears, eyes, mouth, nose*) and ask students to name them. Say, *Touch your nose* and have students copy you. Do this several times slowly, and then say it more quickly so that students have to react fast.

Pre-coding

ACTIVE LEARNING

Sing *Head, shoulders, knees, and toes.*
Materials and preparation
- Audio library – songs
- Flashcards: *ears, eyes, mouth, nose*

Ask students to stand up. Sing *Head, shoulders, knees, and toes* (track 02) and encourage students to sing along and join in with the actions.

Play the verse *my eyes, my ears, my mouth, my nose*, then pause it. Show the flashcards one-by-one and put them on the board in an order different from that mentioned in the verse. Play the verse again and ask students if the order is correct. Help them realize that the flashcards aren't in the correct order.

Listen and stick. Sing.
Materials and preparation
- Audio library – songs
- Project Book page 7

Help students open their Project Book to the stickers page, at the back of their books, and find the stickers for Unit 1. Then help them turn to page 7. Point to the computer and explain that it wants to sing the song, but it doesn't know how to. Remind students that they are "coders" so they are going to teach the computer the correct order so that it can sing the song. Play the verse *my eyes, my ears, my mouth, my nose*, of the *Head, shoulders, knees, and toes* song (track 02) again for students to stick the stickers in the correct order. You may need to play it several times. Help students with the stickers as needed. Check the answers by asking students to hold up their Project Book.

> **Note to teachers**
> Algorithms are instructions that tell a computer how to do a task so that a specific outcome is achieved. In this case, the "outcome" is singing the song correctly, so the "algorithm" says to the computer to sing the parts in the correct order.

My song!
Materials and preparation
- Audio library – songs
- Flashcards: *ears, eyes, mouth, nose* (a set of flashcards per group of four students)

Divide students into groups of four and give each group a set of flashcards. Ask a group to stand up, with each student holding a flashcard. Organize students so that they hold the flashcards in an order different from that of the verse of the song. Encourage students to sing the *Head, shoulders, knees, and toes* song (track 02) again, but this time following the order of the words established for each group.

DIFFERENTIATED INSTRUCTION

BELOW LEVEL
Listen and stick. Sing.
Materials and preparation
- Scissors (teacher's use only)

Cut out the stickers (making sure to leave enough space for them to peel them autonomously) so they can order the stickers off the page first, before sticking them.

ABOVE LEVEL
My song!
Explain to students that they will make their own version of the song and allow them to choose the order of the flashcards.

CLOSING

Spin the bottle. Sing the *Goodbye song.*
Materials and preparation
- A plastic bottle
- Audio library – songs

Have students sit down in a circle. Place the plastic bottle in the middle and spin it. When it stops and lands on a student, ask them to point to a body part by saying, *Touch your (mouth)*.

Alternatively, when the bottle lands on a student, they point to a body part and the other students say what it is.

> **Note to teachers**
> Allow students to spin the bottle, depending on how developed their motor skills are.

Sing the *Goodbye song* (track 05) and invite students to sing along. Say *goodbye* to them and have them say *goodbye* back to you.

Unit 2 How are we all different?

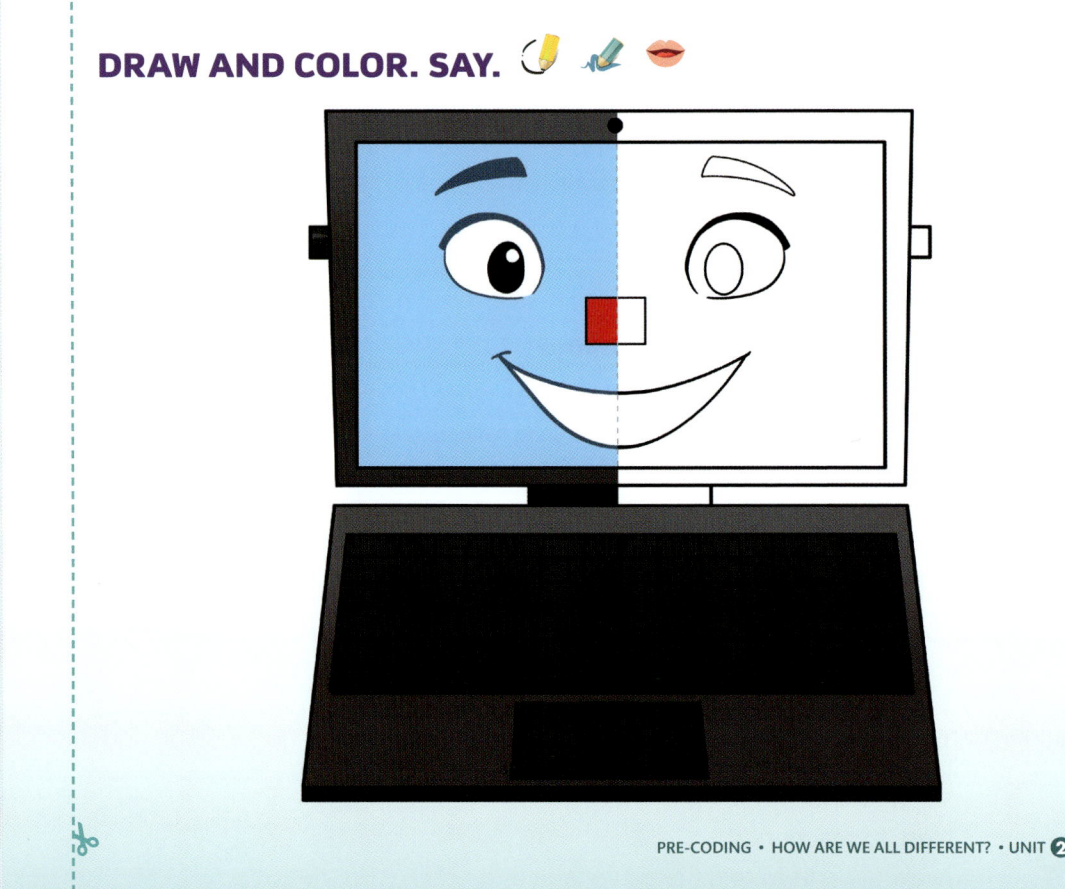

Learning goals
- Complete a symmetrical drawing
- Identify and name parts of the face

Pre-coding skill
- Symmetry

Main language content
Coding: *coder, computer*
Parts of the face: *ears, eyes, nose, mouth*

OPENING

Circle time

Materials and preparation
- Audio library – songs
- Puppet
- Visual schedule pictures

Show the puppet to students and have them greet it with *hello* or *hi*. Sing the *Hello song* (track 04) and have them sing, mime, and dance. Remind students of the attention-getter and practice it with them:
T: *Let's take this road!*
S: *It's time to code!*
or
T: *Turn on your fun mode because it's time to…*
S: *Code!*
Have students sit in a circle. Show them the visual schedule pictures. Choose a class helper of the day and have them order the pictures of the activities as they are mentioned.

> **Note to teachers**
> You can also teach/review the attention-getter *All set? You bet!*

Happy and sad faces

Materials and preparation
- Large printouts or magazine cutouts of happy and sad faces

Show students a printout/magazine cutout of a face. Point to the different parts of the face (*ears, eyes, mouth,* and *nose*) in turn. Ask students to point to the same part of their face and say the word. Then explore the pictures further and encourage students to help you sort them into happy and sad faces.

> **Note to teachers**
> Use gestures to remind students of the meaning of *happy* and *sad*. Ask students to copy you and say the words.

Pre-coding

ACTIVE LEARNING

Symmetry & Me

Ask students to sit in a circle and hold out their hands. Demonstrate putting your hands together (palm to palm), and encourage students to do the same. Help them notice that it is a perfect fit. Then open your hands so your palms are facing upwards and your two pinky fingers are touching each other. Have students copy you. Show them that the fingers are the same, and introduce the concept of symmetry.

Symmetry

Materials and preparation

- Large printouts or magazine cutouts of happy and sad faces
- Large shape cutouts — circles or squares — with a symmetry line drawn and folded in the middle (vertically)

Show students a folded shape cutout and demonstrate opening it, and pointing to the line to show how it is the same on both sides. Pass around the shape cutouts and encourage students to open them and notice that they are the same on both sides. Then show a printout/magazine cutout of a face, and draw a symmetry line down the middle. Count the eyes and ears with students, pointing to your face as necessary. Then point to the nose and mouth, helping students notice the symmetry.

Draw and color. Say.

Materials and preparation

- Crayons
- Pencils
- Project Book page 9

Help students open their Project Book to page 9. Point to the picture and ask students to name it. Remind them that they are coders and they help the computer do things. Help students draw the symmetry line down the middle of the computer. Then give them time to color the computer. When they have finished, ask, *Is the computer happy or sad?*

DIFFERENTIATED INSTRUCTION

BELOW LEVEL
Draw and color. Say.

Materials and preparation

- Rulers

Support students as they draw the symmetry line by holding a ruler on the page.

ABOVE LEVEL
Draw and color. Say.

Students can draw other features on the computer, and then copy these across to the other side to make a symmetrical drawing.

CLOSING

Combine the blocks. Sing the *Goodbye song*.

Materials and preparation

- Audio library – songs
- Building blocks
- Masking tape

Make a vertical line on the floor with masking tape. Put building blocks on one side, in different combinations (no stacking), e.g. one red block, one yellow block, and two green blocks. Invite students to put the same blocks on the other side of the line. Help them notice that the sides are symmetrical.

> **Note to teachers**
> Use this opportunity to review with students the words for colors.

Sing the *Goodbye song* (track 05) and invite students to sing along. Say *goodbye* to them and have them say *goodbye* back to you.

Unit 2 | 13

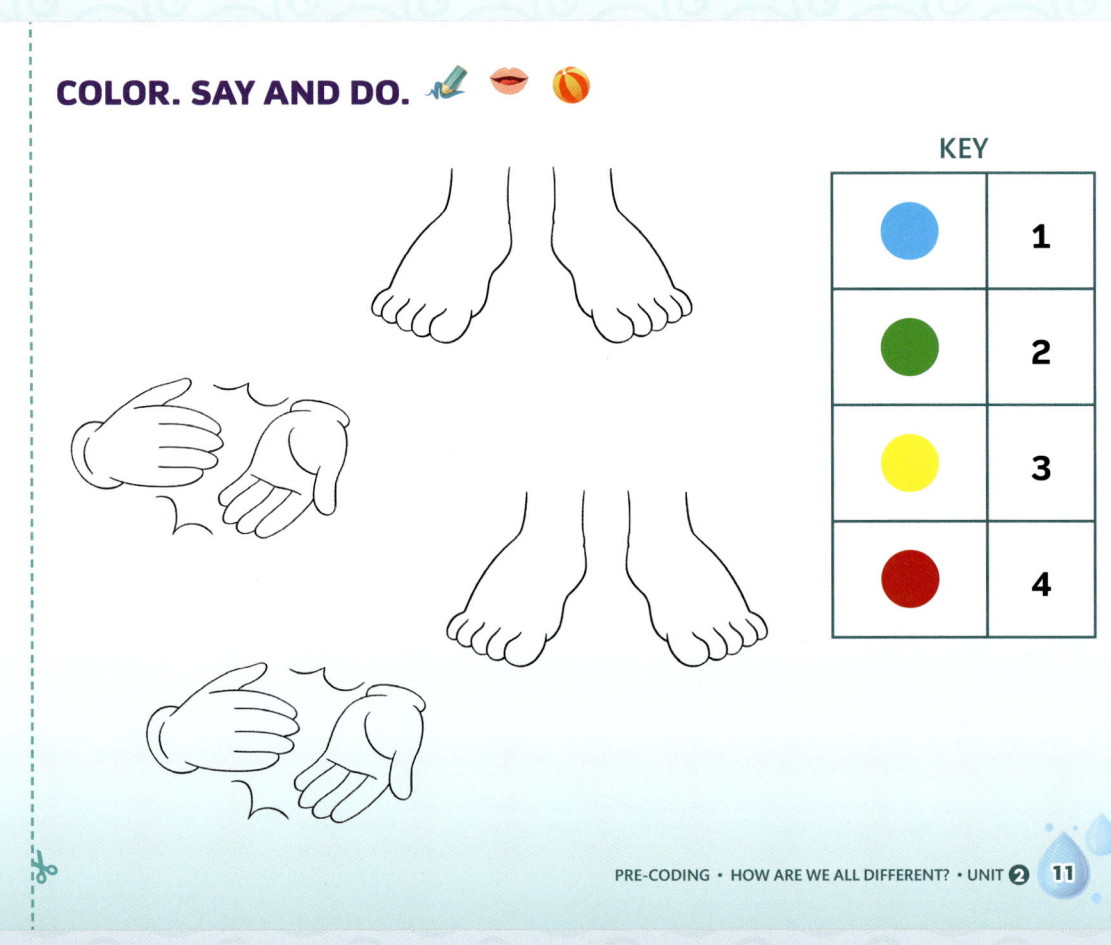

Learning goals
- Teach and do a repeated sequence of actions
- Recognize and use words for numbers and body parts

Pre-coding skill
- Looping

Main language content
Actions: *clap your hands, stamp your feet*
Numbers: *1–4*
Parts of the body: *feet, hands*

OPENING

Circle time

Materials and preparation
- Puppet
- Visual schedule pictures (hide them around the classroom)

Show the puppet to students and have them greet it with *hello* or *hi*. Remind students of the attention-getter and practice it with them:
T: *Let's take this road!*
S: *It's time to code!*
or
T: *Turn on your fun mode because it's time to…*
S: *Code!*
Hide the visual schedule pictures that refer to today's activities. Tell students to look for them around the classroom. As they find a picture, tell them to hand it to you. Then talk to students about each of the moments of the class.

> **Note to teachers**
> Remind students that they should be quiet and pay attention when you use the attention-getter.

Happy or sad?

Review the numbers with students by clapping one to five together, and asking students to clap more quietly, louder, etc. Then review *happy* and *sad* using gestures. Assign a number of claps to *happy* and a number to *sad*. Make a happy or sad face, and encourage students to say *happy* or *sad*, and clap the correct number of times. Invite individual students to stand up and make a happy/sad face for the other students to identify and clap accordingly. Then repeat the activity using *stamp your feet* and other numbers.

ACTIVE LEARNING

Sing *If you're happy and you know it*.

Materials and preparation
- Audio library – songs

Ask students to stand up and make a circle. Teach them a simple set of actions, e.g., jump, spin around, and clap. Practice a few times. Play the song *If you're happy and you know it* (track 07), while students walk/skip/dance around in a circle. When you pause the music, students do the set of actions repeatedly until you play the music again, and they can start walking, skip, again. Repeat this procedure for some time. You should set up expectations of moving safely so as to avoid accidents.

Color. Say and do.

Materials and preparation
- Crayons: blue, green, red, and yellow
- Project Book page 11

Help students open their Project Book to page 11. Point to the pictures and ask them to say the words. Give out the crayons and point to the key on the right of the page. Ask students to show you the corresponding crayon, as you point to each color and say its name. Give them some time to color the pictures as they choose the order of the actions (clap your hands, stamp your feet). Monitor and help as needed. When they have finished, help students say the colors in their loop. Then organize them into pairs and ask them to teach the sequence of actions to their classmate. The second student does the actions until the first student says *stop*. Then pairs can switch roles.

> **Note to teacher**
> Make sure to join in with students as they teach and do.

DIFFERENTIATED INSTRUCTION

BELOW LEVEL
Color. Say and do.

Students can choose the order of the actions in pairs.

ABOVE LEVEL
Color. Say and do.

Students work independently and can create other sequences of actions.

CLOSING

Play *You are computers*. Sing the *Goodbye song*.

Materials and preparation
- Audio library – songs

Play *You are computers* with students. Explain to students that now they are "computers" and you are the "coder". Say two or three actions (e.g. *Clap your hands. Stamp your feet. Clap your hands.*) and have students do the actions in sequence until you say *stop*.
Sing the *Goodbye song* (track 05) and invite students to sing along. Say *goodbye* to them and have them say *goodbye* back to you.

Unit 3 What is a family?

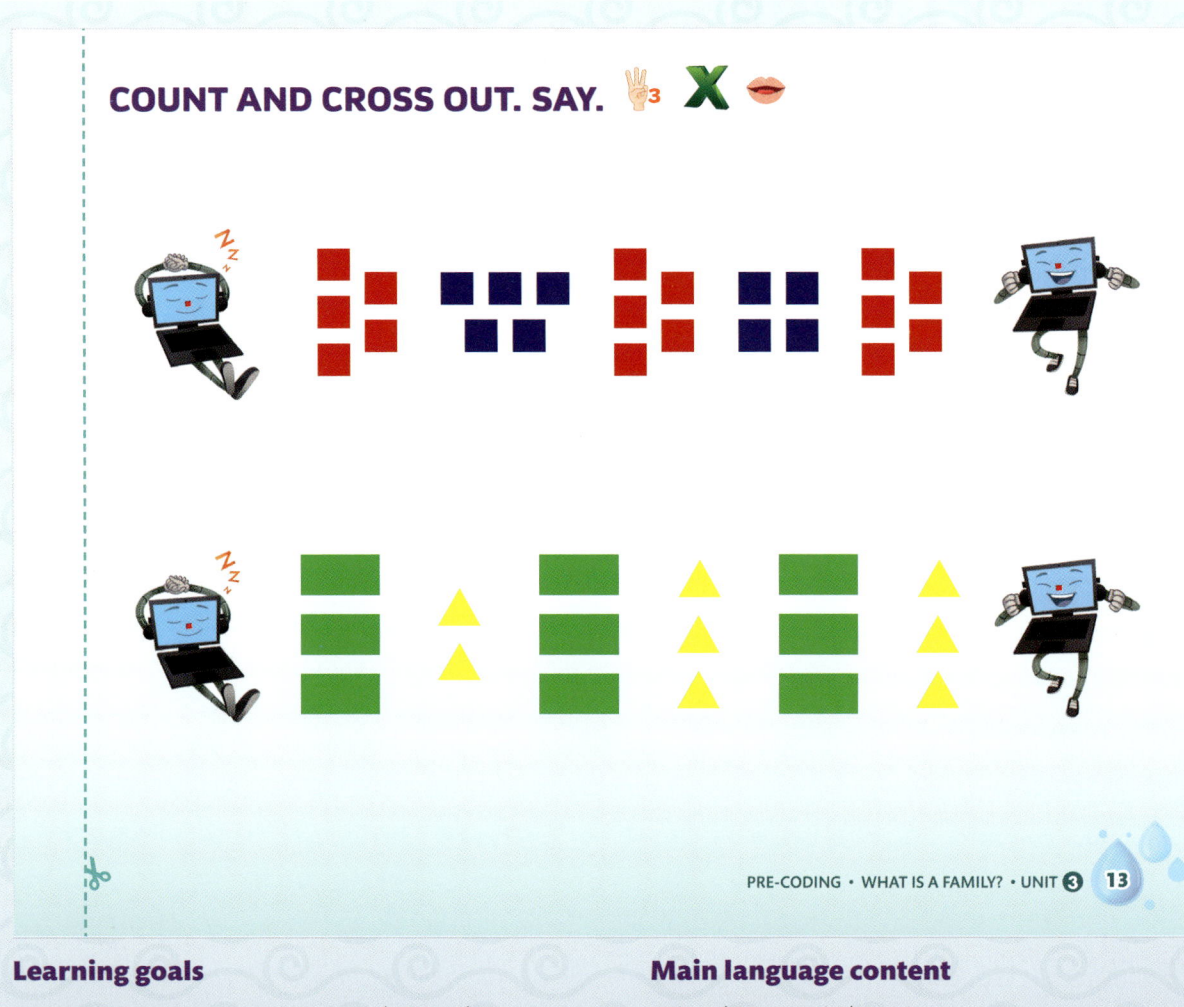

Learning goals
- Identify an incorrect element (a "bug") in a sequence
- Count to five

Pre-coding skill
- Debugging

Main language content
What (shape/color) is it?
Coding: *bug*
Colors: *blue, green, red, yellow*
Shapes: *circle, rectangle, square, triangle*
Numbers: *1–5*

OPENING

Circle time

Materials and preparation
- Audio library – songs
- Puppet
- Visual schedule pictures

Show the puppet to students and have them greet it with *hello* or *hi*. Sing the *Hello song* (track 04) and have them sing, mime, and dance. Remind students of the attention-getter and practice it with them:
T: *Let's take this road!*
S: *It's time to code!*
or
T: *Turn on your fun mode because it's time to...*
S: *Code!*
Have students sit in a circle. Show each visual schedule picture and then separate the ones that show the activities of today's class. Have a volunteer place the activities in the middle of the circle.

> **Note to teachers**
> You can also teach/review the attention-getter *All set? You bet!*

Categorizing colors and shapes

Materials and preparation
- Building blocks: blue, green, red, and yellow
- Plastic shapes

Ask students to sit in a circle. Spread the building blocks and plastic shapes in the middle of the circle. Invite students to categorize the materials by color and shape. Review the colors, shapes, and numbers with students by asking individual/pairs of students to take specific numbers/colors/shapes, e.g. *Give me two red blocks, please.*

> **Note to teachers**
> Make sure to praise students for correctly identifying colors, shapes, etc.

ACTIVE LEARNING

Play *Musical statues*.

Materials and preparation
- Audio library – songs (or another song students like)
- Small pictures of bugs with double-sided tape stuck on the back

Ask students to stand up and play *Musical statues*. Play a song from the audio library (or another song that students like), and pause it occasionally for students to stand as still as possible until you start the music again. Model the game. When you pause the song, stick a picture of a bug on your shirt and walk around the students trying to distract them. Say, *I'm a bug!* If a student moves, stick a picture of a bug on their shirt. Play the song again. During the next statue time, the "bug" student can walk around the "statues", trying to distract them (but without touching them). You should set up expectations of walking safely so as to avoid accidents. After the activity, talk to students and help them understand that the "bugs" didn't do the correct thing when they tried to prevent other students from participating correctly in the game.

Count and cross out. Say.

Materials and preparation
- Crayons
- Project Book page 13

Help students open their Project Book to page 13. Point to the first sequence and ask, *What shape is it? What color is it?* Students say the shape and the color. Help students count the shapes and identify the number of each one. When you get to the end of the first sequence, go back to the four blue squares and count them again. Say, *Uh-oh, it's different! It's a bug!* and help them cross out the four blue squares. Then repeat with the second sequence, but this time encourage students to count and identify the "bug" with less interference from you.

> **Note to teachers**
> In coding, a "bug" is a mistake that prevents something from functioning correctly. This activity helps students associate this via pictures; they notice that the incorrect picture spoils the sequence.

DIFFERENTIATED INSTRUCTION

BELOW LEVEL
Count and cross out. Say.

Materials and preparation
- Building blocks

Replicate the activity using building blocks to help students with the counting.

ABOVE LEVEL
Count and cross out. Say.

Materials and preparation
- Crayons
- Sheets of paper

Students can draw the correct sequence (without the "bug") on a separate sheet of paper.

CLOSING

Find the bug! Sing the *Goodbye song*.

Materials and preparation
- Audio library – songs
- Buttons (different sizes and colors)

Have students sit in a circle. In the middle, make a sequence of buttons in which one of them is different. Invite students to take out the "bug" to correct the pattern.
Sing the *Goodbye song* (track 05) and invite students to sing along. Say *goodbye* to them and have them say *goodbye* back to you.

> **Note to teachers**
> Allow the confident students to help you make the pattern.

LOOK AND STICK.

PRE-CODING • WHAT IS A FAMILY? • UNIT 3 — 15

Learning goals
- Recognize and complete a pattern
- Identify and practice using words for family members

Pre-coding skill
- Patterns

Main language content
Who is this?
Actions: *clap, jump, stop*
Colors: *blue, green, red, yellow*
Family: *baby, brother, daddy, mommy, sister*

OPENING

Circle time

Materials and preparation
- Puppet
- Visual schedule pictures

Show the puppet to students and have them greet it with *hello* or *hi*. Remind students of the attention-getter and practice it with them:
T: *Let's take this road!*
S: *It's time to code!*
or
T: *Turn on your fun mode because it's time to…*
S: *Code!*
Show students the visual schedule pictures. Ask for volunteers to help you turn them over. Encourage the whole class to say what each picture shows. Ask students to help you select the pictures that show today's schedule as you tell them what they are going to do today.

> **Note to teachers**
> Remind students that they should be quiet and pay attention when you use the attention-getter.

Play *Clap, jump, stop!*

Materials and preparation
- Audio library – songs

Play a song from the audio library as students run or dance around in a circle. Pause the music and call out *clap, jump,* or *stop*. Students do the actions. Repeat this several times. Then have students sit down in a circle and reflect on the game. Ask them to tell/show you the sequence of the actions. You should set up expectations of moving safely so as to avoid accidents.

18 Pre-coding

ACTIVE LEARNING

Making patterns

Materials and preparation
- Snap cubes or blocks: blue, green, red, and yellow

Divide students into pairs or small groups, sitting in a circle. Give each pair/group four green cubes/blocks and four yellow cubes/blocks. Say, *A (green) cube/block* and have students pick one. Then say, *A (yellow) cube/block* and have students attach it to the previous blocks. Repeat this several times until students have made a two-color pattern. Then ask students to point to the blocks and recognize the pattern.

> **Note to teachers**
> Patterns are important in coding as unknown/incorrect patterns help coders identify problems.

Look and stick.

Materials and preparation
- Project Book page 15

Help students open their Project Book to page 15. Point to each picture and ask, *Who is this?* Have students say the words for the family members. Help them recognize the pattern and then go to the stickers page at the back of the book. Help them peel off the stickers for Unit 3, and stick them in the correct squares on page 15. Monitor and help as needed.

DIFFERENTIATED INSTRUCTION

BELOW LEVEL
Look and stick.

Go over the patterns with students and help them identify what comes next.

ABOVE LEVEL
Look and stick.

Materials and preparation
- Crayons and colored pencils
- Sheets of paper

Students can draw the next picture in the pattern to continue it on a separate sheet of paper.

CLOSING

Create a pattern. Sing the *Goodbye song*.

Materials and preparation
- Audio library – songs
- Flashcards: *blue, green, red, yellow* (a copy of a flashcard per student)

Ask students to stand up. Give each student a flashcard to hold up in front of them. Work with students to create a pattern of colors. They should arrange themselves, holding their flashcards in front of them.

> **Note to teachers**
> If possible, take a picture of students' patterns for the classroom display.

Sing the *Goodbye song* (track 05) and invite students to sing along. Say *goodbye* to them and have them say *goodbye* back to you.

Unit 4 Do you share your toys?

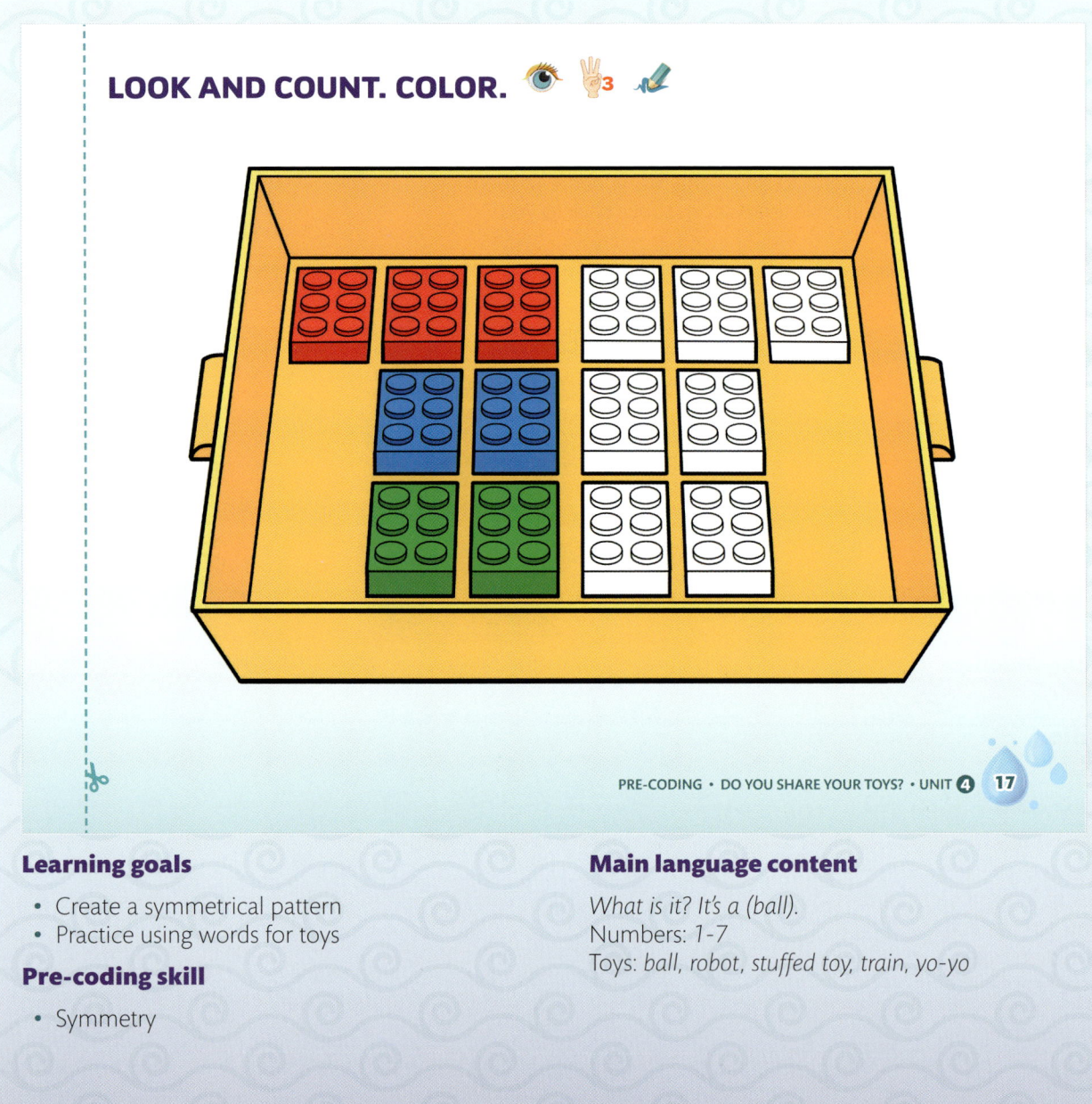

Learning goals
- Create a symmetrical pattern
- Practice using words for toys

Pre-coding skill
- Symmetry

Main language content
What is it? It's a (ball).
Numbers: 1-7
Toys: ball, robot, stuffed toy, train, yo-yo

OPENING

Circle time

Materials and preparation
- Audio library – songs
- Puppet
- Visual schedule pictures

Show the puppet to students and have them greet it with *hello* or *hi*. Sing the *Hello song* (track 04) and have them sing, mime, and dance. Remind students of the attention-getter and practice it with them:
T: *Let's take this road!*
S: *It's time to code!*
or
T: *Turn on your fun mode because it's time to…*
S: *Code!*
Have students sit in a circle. Show them the visual schedule pictures. Ask for volunteers to help you turn them over. Encourage the whole class to say what each picture shows. Choose a class helper of the day and have them order the pictures of the activities as they are mentioned.

> **Note to teachers**
> You can also teach/review the attention-getter *All set? You bet!*

A bag of toys

Materials and preparation
- A bag filled with toys that students are familiar with (if possible, one per student)

Ask students to sit in a circle. Pass the bag to the first student on your right. Ask them to take out a toy and say what it is. Encourage the other students to help out with the vocabulary, if the student doesn't know the name of the toy. Use L1 as needed. Continue until all the students have had the chance to take out a toy and say its name.
If you don't have enough toys, the student can put the toy back into the bag after they say its name.

> **Note to teachers**
> At the end of the activity, you could put all of the toys in the middle of the circle and invite each student to point to their favorite toy.

ACTIVE LEARNING

Find the blocks.

Materials and preparation

- Blocks or any other small objects (at least ten; eight of which are the same color — hide them around the classroom.)

Ask ten volunteers to walk around and find the hidden objects. When they are back in the circle, ask students to separate the objects according to their color.

Look and count. Color.

Materials and preparation

- Crayons: blue, green, and red
- Project Book page 17

Help students open their Project Book to page 17. Point to the colored blocks on the left side of the toy box and count the blocks together (there are seven in total). Then point to the red blocks and count them together. Help students identify the corresponding blocks on the right side of the toy box. Give them time to color the three blocks red. Repeat with the other blocks. When they have finished, explore the picture and help them notice that it is the same on each side.

DIFFERENTIATED INSTRUCTION

BELOW LEVEL
Look and count. Color.

Help students notice the pattern by modeling the activity. Point to a red block on the left side of the toy box, then point to the corresponding block on the right side. Give students time to color. Repeat with the other blocks.

ABOVE LEVEL
Look and count. Color.

Encourage students to notice the pattern and color autonomously.

CLOSING

Find the same shoes. Sing the *Goodbye song*.

Materials and preparation

- A selection of pairs of shoes
- Audio library – songs

Spread out the shoes in the middle of the classroom. In pairs, students find a matching pair of shoes and place them side by side. Encourage them to walk around their classmates' shoes, noticing how they are the same (symmetry).
Sing the *Goodbye song* (track 05) and invite students to sing along. Say *goodbye* to them and have them say *goodbye* back to you.

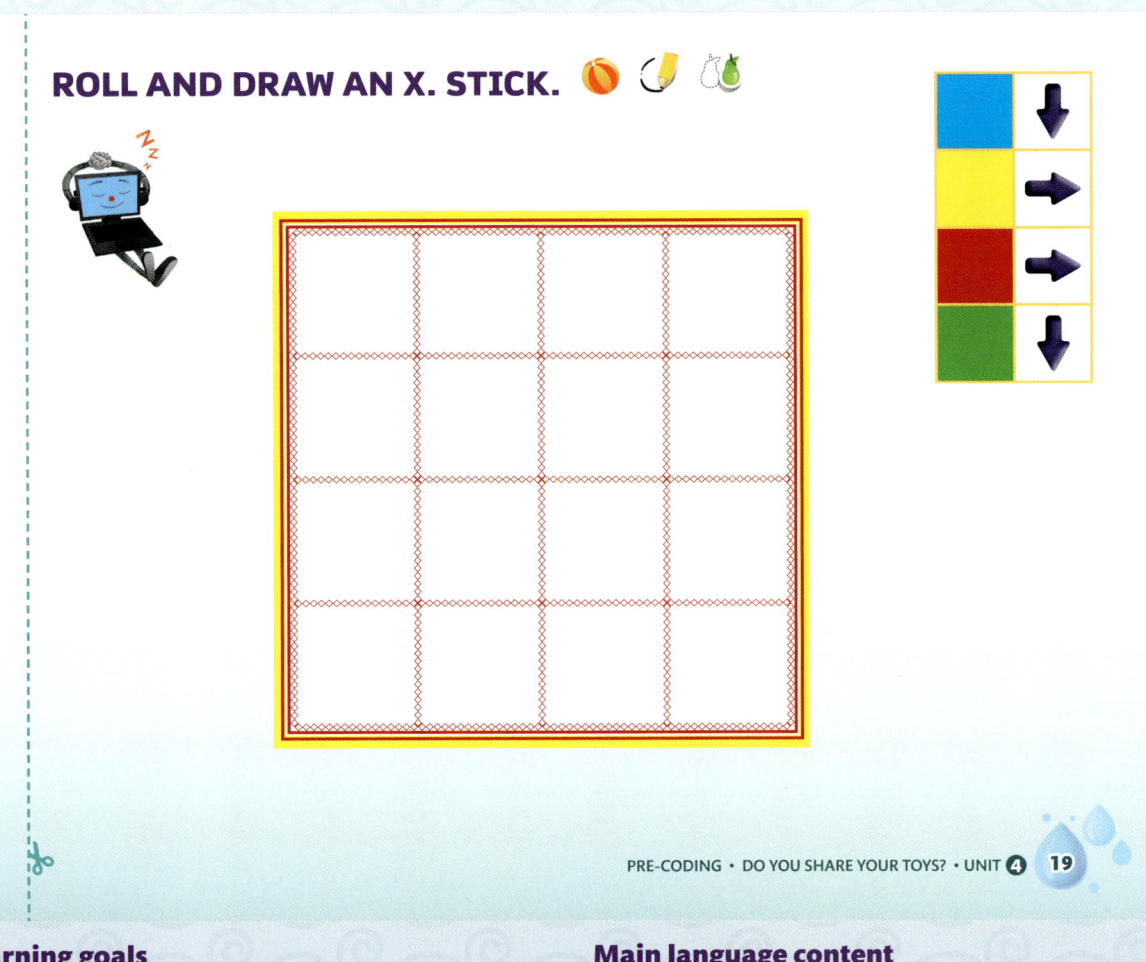

Learning goals
- Match conditions with results
- Identify and follow commands

Pre-coding skill
- Branching (If-Then)

Main language content
Coding: *computer*
Colors: *blue, green, red, yellow*
Directions: *across, down*
Feelings: *happy, sad*

OPENING

Circle time

Materials and preparation
- Puppet
- Visual schedule pictures (hide them around the classroom)

Show the puppet to students and have them greet it with *hello* or *hi*. Remind students of the attention-getter and practice it with them:
T: *Let's take this road!*
S: *It's time to code!*
or
T: *Turn on your fun mode because it's time to…*
S: *Code!*
Hide the visual schedule pictures that refer to today's activities. Tell students to look for them around the classroom. As they find a picture, tell them to hand it to you. Then talk to students about each of the moments of the class.

> **Note to teachers**
> Remind students that they should be quiet and pay attention when you use the attention-getter.

Follow the commands.

Materials and preparation
- Audio library – songs (or another song students like)
- Flashcards: *blue, green, red, yellow*
- Two large sheets of paper (red and yellow)

Stick the red sheet of paper on a wall, and the yellow sheet on an opposite wall. Show the red flashcard and encourage students to run to the red wall. Repeat with the yellow flashcard. Show the blue and green flashcards, say the word *down*, and demonstrate lying on the ground or crouching down and have students copy you.
Play a song from the audio library or any other song that students like. Encourage them to dance around. Pause the music and show a flashcard; students either run to the corresponding wall or lie

down on the floor. Repeat this several times. You should set up expectations of walking safely so as to avoid accidents.

> **Note to teachers**
> This activity introduces the coding concept of "if-then", which means that if a specific command is given, a specific task is completed. In this activity, this is very simple: if you show a certain colored flashcard, students do a specific action.

ACTIVE LEARNING

Roll and draw an X. Stick.

Materials and preparation
- Buttons or other small objects to use as counters (optional)
- Flashcards: *blue, green, red, yellow* (optional)
- Pencils
- Project Book page 19
- Students' color dice (from Unit 1)

Help students open their Project Book to page 19. Give out students' color dice. Call out the colors and ask them to show the correct side of the die. Point to the key and help students understand the direction of the arrows by holding up the flashcards and moving in the corresponding direction. Give each student several buttons or counters. Help students roll their dice. Depending on the color they land on, they draw an X in the square. For example, if they land on blue, they draw an X in the square down. When students have reached the end of the grid, help them go to the stickers page at the back of the book, peel off the dancing computer (Unit 4), and stick it next to the place they left the grid. Help them with the stickers as needed. Alternatively, instead of drawing an X in the squares, students can place a button/counter and draw the Xs after placing the sticker.

According to students' development, this activity can be done in different ways: 1) as a whole group, with volunteer students rolling their dice and telling the class the number it lands on; 2) in small groups, with students taking turns rolling their dice to get the color; 3) individually, with a lot of support from you or assistants.

If you don't have the dice from Unit 1, you can use the colors flashcards. Spread the flashcards face down on your desk and ask one student at a time to choose one of them. They turn the flashcard over, say the name of the color and all the students should color the square that color. Then ask another student to turn another flashcard, and so on.

> **Note to teachers**
> When students have finished, they can show each other their completed grids.

DIFFERENTIATED INSTRUCTION

BELOW LEVEL
Roll and draw an X. Stick.

Materials and preparation
- Glue (optional)
- Play dough (optional)
- Stickers of simple shapes

Students can place stickers on the squares instead of marking with a pencil. Alternatively they can make small balls of play dough and glue them in the squares.

ABOVE LEVEL
Roll and draw an X. Stick.

Students can draw an X on the squares straight away, without placing the counters.

CLOSING

Role-play being coders and computers. Sing the *Goodbye song*.

Materials and preparation
- A kitchen timer/egg timer/online chronometer app (optional)
- Audio library – songs

Tell students that they are "computers", and ask a volunteer student to be the "coder". The "coder" stands in front of the "computers". The "computers" have to mimic everything that that the "coder" does. You may like to set a timer and switch the "coder" when the timer runs out.

> **Note to teachers**
> This is another simple example of an "if-then" command.

Sing the *Goodbye song* (track 05) and invite students to sing along. Say *goodbye* to them and have them say *goodbye* back to you.

Unit 5 How do you help at home?

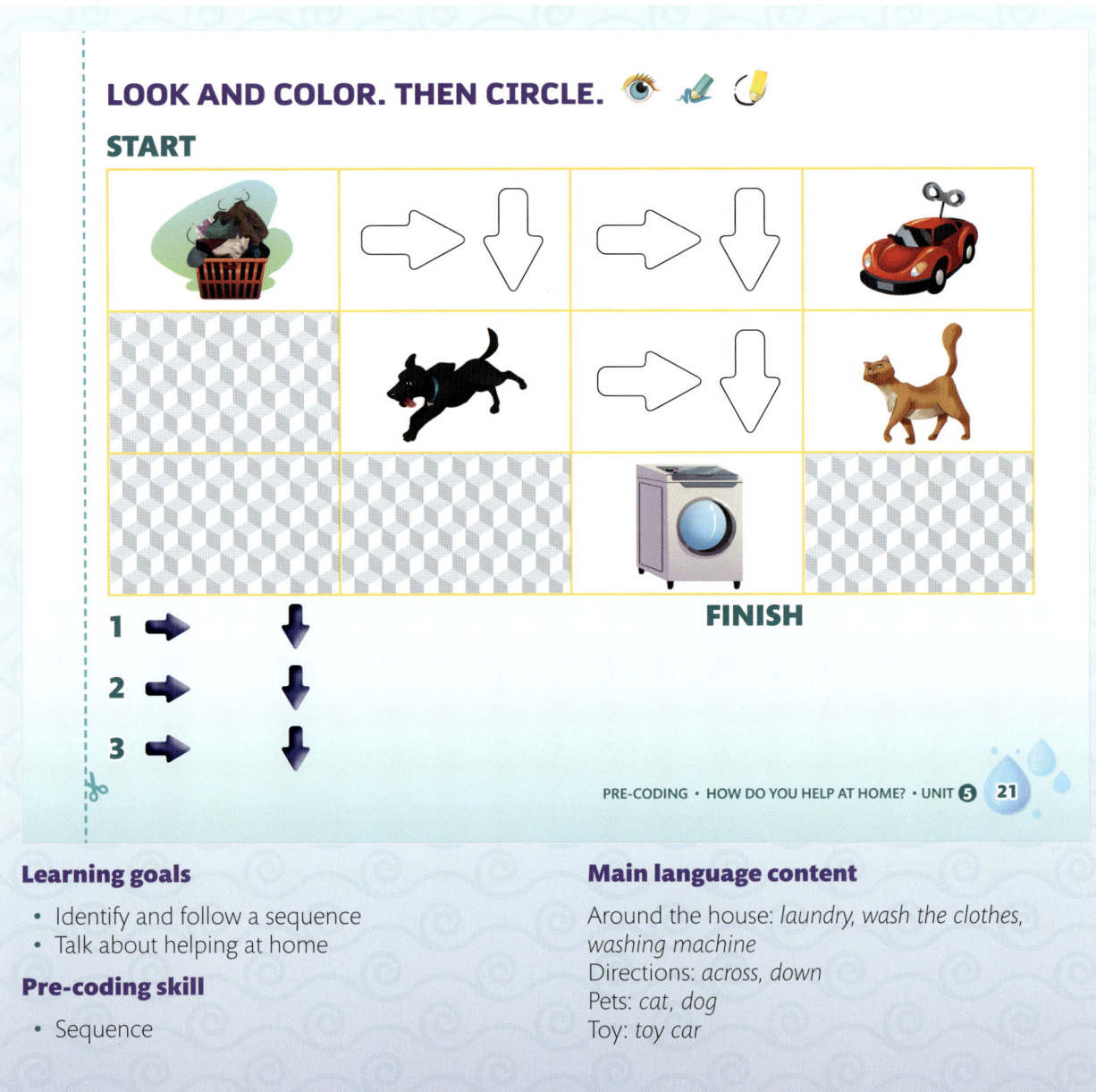

OPENING

Circle time

Materials and preparation
- Audio library – songs
- Puppet
- Visual schedule pictures

Show the puppet to students and have them greet it with *hello* or *hi*. Sing the *Hello song* (track 04) and have them sing, mime, and dance. Remind students of the attention-getter and practice it with them:
T: *Let's take this road!*
S: *It's time to code!*
or
T: *Turn on your fun mode because it's time to…*
S: *Code!*
Have students sit in a circle. Show them the visual schedule pictures. Ask for volunteers to help you turn them over. Encourage the whole class to say what each picture shows. Choose a class helper of the day and have them order the pictures of the activities as they are mentioned.

> **Note to teachers**
> You can also teach/review the attention-getter *All set? You bet!*

Sing *The mop song*.

Materials and preparation
- Audio library – songs

Sing *The mop song* (track 13). Ask students to stand up, sing along, and do the actions.

Learning goals
- Identify and follow a sequence
- Talk about helping at home

Pre-coding skill
- Sequence

Main language content
Around the house: *laundry, wash the clothes, washing machine*
Directions: *across, down*
Pets: *cat, dog*
Toy: *toy car*

24 Pre-coding

ACTIVE LEARNING

Clean up the clothes.

Materials and preparation
- Cards with the numbers one to five written on it (one set per every five students)
- Clean rags/small towels (one per student)
- Laundry baskets, boxes, or buckets (one per every five students)

Divide students into groups of five. Show the cards and ask students to identify and say each number. Stick a card on each student's T-shirt. Ask them to stand up in a line in the correct order. Show the rags/towels and tell students that these are the dirty clothes. They have to pick them up, run to the basket (or box/bucket), and drop in the clothes. One student runs at a time and when all students have finished, they sit down. You should set up expectations of walking safely so as to avoid accidents.

After the game has finished, ask students to take off their cards and lay the sequence on the ground. You could ask each group to count up to five, pointing to the numbers.

> **Note to teachers**
> In this activity, students should stay in numerical order, thus familiarizing them with the idea of sequences.

Look and color. Then circle.

Materials and preparation
- Pencils
- Project Book page 21
- Two sheets of paper, one with a sideways arrow → and one with a down arrow ↓

Show to students the sideways arrow, and say *across* as you take a step to the right. Have them repeat the word and the action after you. Show the down arrow and say *down* as you crouch down. Repeat this several times with students copying you to help them understand the meaning of the words.

Help students open their Project Book to page 21. Point to the picture of the dirty laundry and ask students to identify it. Ask, *What do we do with dirty laundry?*, encourage students to respond with ideas about washing clothes, and then point to the washing machine. Explain that they need to take the dirty laundry to the washing machine while avoiding the "obstacles" by coloring the correct arrow. Copy the grid onto the board and work through it with students. Ask them which arrow they need first to move toward the washing machine. Then repeat the procedure twice so that they can understand the sequence of the arrows they need to color. Once students have colored the correct arrow in each square, they circle them at the bottom of the page to show the "code".

DIFFERENTIATED INSTRUCTION

BELOW LEVEL
Look and color. Then circle.

Do the activity with students. Point to each arrow, ask them to point to the appropriate direction and help them notice which arrow to color. Then have them look at the bottom of the page and help them recognize which arrow they have to circle.

ABOVE LEVEL
Look and color. Then circle.

Allow students to work more autonomously. Ask them which arrow they have to color and circle.

CLOSING

Follow the commands. Sing the *Goodbye song*.

Materials and preparation
- Audio library – songs
- Masking tape
- Two or three toys

Draw a similar grid on the floor using masking tape. Draw an X for the start and finish squares. Add a toy to some of the squares to serve as obstacles. One student stands in the grid, while their classmates try to guide them to the finish square. Students can call out *across* or *down* according to the direction. Alternatively, you can use the grid you have drawn on the board, but this time draw the obstacles in different squares. Have students call out *across* or *down* to get to the finish square.

> **Note to teachers**
> Make sure that the start and finish squares are positioned so that students only move to the right, as they are not expected to know the concepts of left and right.

Sing the *Goodbye song* (track 05) and invite students to sing along. Say *goodbye* to them and have them say *goodbye* back to you.

Unit 5 | 25

COUNT AND COLOR.

PRE-CODING • HOW DO YOU HELP AT HOME? • UNIT 5   23

Learning goals
- Break down a large number into smaller ones
- Identify and practice saying numbers up to nine

Pre-coding skill
- Decomposition

Main language content
How many?
Clothes: *shorts, socks, T-shirt*
Numbers: *1-9*

OPENING

Circle time

Materials and preparation
- Puppet
- Visual schedule pictures

Show the puppet to students and have them greet it with *hello* or *hi*. Remind students of the attention-getter and practice it with them:
T: *Let's take this road!*
S: *It's time to code!*
or
T: *Turn on your fun mode because it's time to…*
S: *Code!*
Show students the visual schedule pictures. Ask for volunteers to help you turn them over. Encourage the whole class to say what each picture shows. Ask students to help you select the pictures that show today's schedule as you tell them what they are going to do today.

> **Note to teachers**
> Remind students that they should be quiet and pay attention when you use the attention-getter.

Sorting the laundry

Materials and preparation
- A laundry basket (or large box)
- A selection of T-shirts, socks, and shorts (no more than nine per item type)

Show students the clothes in the laundry basket. Ask them to identify the colors of the clothes and to identify the different types. You can teach the words *T-shirt*, *socks*, and *shorts*, but only for the purpose of this activity — do not spend too much time on this. Tell students that the clothes are dirty and you need to wash them, but there are a lot of clothes and you need to sort them to make the task easier. Invite students to help you sort the clothes by type or by color. Use L1 as needed.

Pre-coding

Note to teachers
Allowing students to decide how to sort the clothes helps them develop autonomy.

ACTIVE LEARNING

Count and color.

Materials and preparation
- Crayons
- Project Book page 23

Help students open their Project Book to page 23. Ask them what they can see in the picture. Explain that they have to hang out the laundry, but there is a lot in the basket. Ask them how they can hang it out to make it easier. Tell them they can do it by type, for example. Point to the T-shirts, and help students count them aloud. Ask students to color the T-shirts in the basket. Then repeat with the other items of clothing. Finally, ask students to color the corresponding items of clothing on the washing line.

Note to teachers
In coding, decomposition refers to breaking a bigger task into small, more manageable tasks in order to achieve a desired result. In this activity, students practice this skill through simulating hanging out clean laundry – they break down the task into smaller tasks by hanging out clothes by type.

DIFFERENTIATED INSTRUCTION

BELOW LEVEL
Count and color.

Assign a color to each item of clothing to reduce students' anxiety and allow them to focus only on the task of sorting/coloring.

ABOVE LEVEL
Count and color.

More confident students can take the lead when choosing how to sort the clothes.

CLOSING

Clean up! Sing the *Goodbye song*.

Materials and preparation
- Audio library – songs
- Classroom objects (crayons, toys, etc.)

Spread out some crayons and toys around the classroom. Tell students, *Look at this mess! We need to clean up!* Help students work out how to make this more manageable, for example, some students can pick up the crayons, some students can pick up the toys, and other students can put these in the toy box. They work together to clean up the classroom.
Sing the *Goodbye song* (track 05) and invite students to sing along. Say *goodbye* to them and have them say *goodbye* back to you.

Unit 6 How do you take care of your pet?

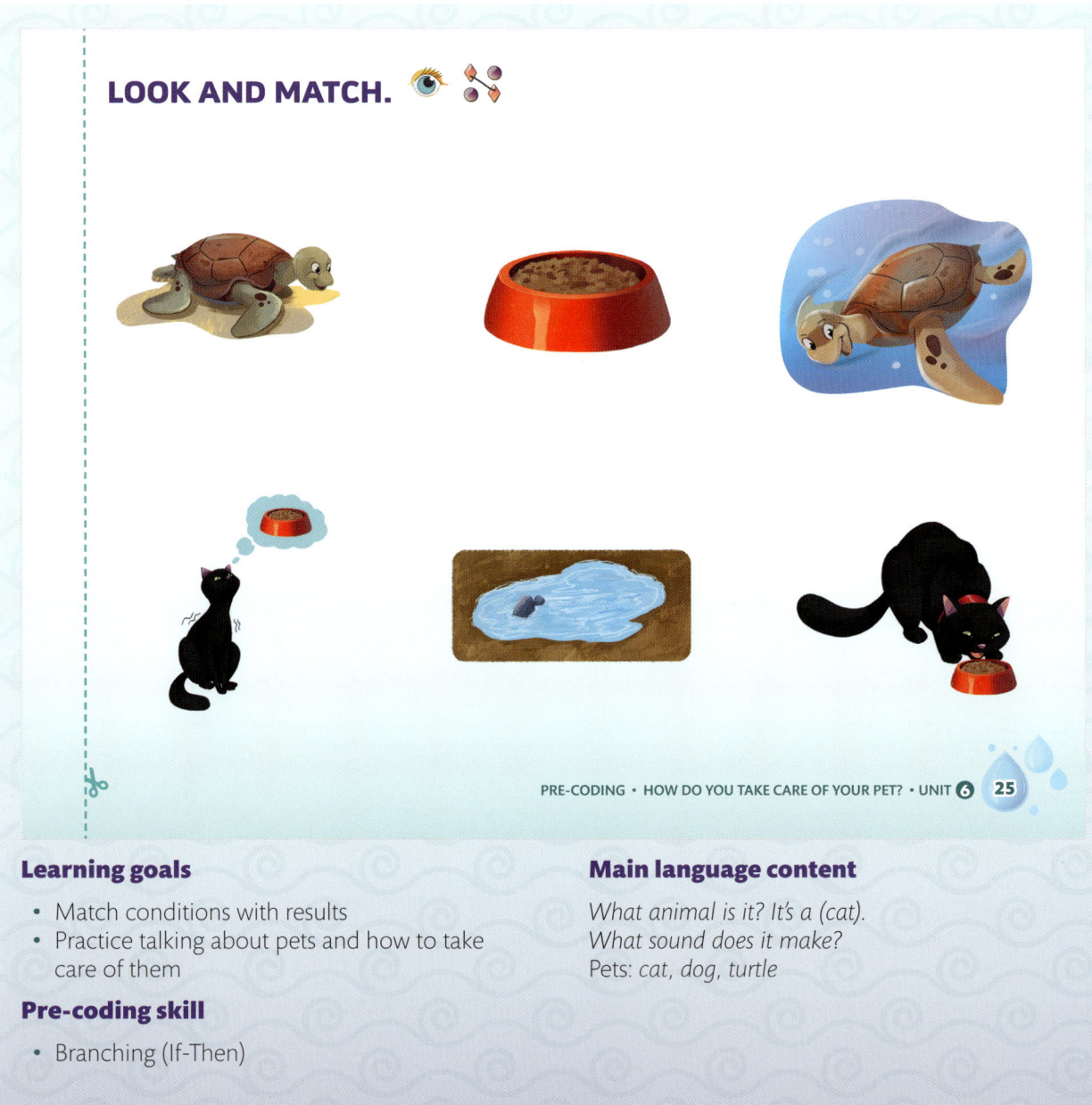

Learning goals
- Match conditions with results
- Practice talking about pets and how to take care of them

Pre-coding skill
- Branching (If-Then)

Main language content

What animal is it? It's a (cat).
What sound does it make?
Pets: cat, dog, turtle

OPENING

Circle time

Materials and preparation
- Audio library – songs
- Puppet
- Visual schedule pictures

Show the puppet to students and have them greet it with *hello* or *hi*. Sing the *Hello song* (track 04) and have them sing, mime, and dance. Remind students of the attention-getter and practice it with them:
T: *Let's take this road!*
S: *It's time to code!*
or
T: *Turn on your fun mode because it's time to…*
S: *Code!*
Have students sit in a circle. Show them the visual schedule pictures. Ask for volunteers to help you turn them over. Encourage the whole class to say what each picture shows. Choose a class helper of the day and have them order the pictures of the activities as they are mentioned.

> **Note to teachers**
> You can also teach/review the attention-getter *All set? You bet!*

Sing *Why is that doggie in the window?*

Materials and preparation
- Audio library – songs

Sing *Why is that doggie in the window?* (track 21). Ask students to stand up, sing along, and do the actions.

ACTIVE LEARNING

Play *Animal sounds*.

Materials and preparation
- Pictures of animals that students know/recognize

Play *Animal sounds* with students. Show them the pictures of the animals one by one and ask, *What sound does it make?* Encourage students to make the sound. Show the pictures in random order and have students make the sound when they see the picture.

> **Note to teachers**
> The focus of this activity isn't to teach students the animal words, but to help them understand that if you show a certain picture, then they make a specific sound.

Look and match.

Materials and preparation
- Crayons: two different colors
- Project Book page 25

Help students open their Project Book to page 25. Have them take a look at the page. Point to the first picture and ask, *What animal is it?* Then repeat with the next picture. Ask, *How is the animal feeling?* Help them think about how they could make things better for the animal. Then help students identify the appropriate thing they should offer to each animal to make them feel better. Ask them to use different colors for each animal. Help them draw the lines, if necessary.

Explore the pictures together by saying, for example, *Look at the cat. It's hungry. If we give it food, then it can eat and it isn't hungry anymore!*

> **Note to teachers**
> This activity practices branching, because students see that if they give an animal a specific condition, then something will happen.

DIFFERENTIATED INSTRUCTION

BELOW LEVEL
Look and match.

Give students plenty of help with identifying the pictures and drawing the lines.

ABOVE LEVEL
Look and match.

Students can work more autonomously. Point to the first picture and ask them, *What's wrong?* Then have students identify the solution for each situation and match the pictures.

CLOSING

Take care of your animal. Sing the *Goodbye song*.

Materials and preparation
- Audio library – songs
- Stuffed animals toys

Give out the stuffed toys again and ask students what they can do to take care of their animals. Encourage them to explain to the rest of the group. Use L1 as needed. Sing the *Goodbye song* (track 05) and invite students to sing along. Say *goodbye* to them and have them say *goodbye* back to you.

Learning goals
- Identify an incorrect element (a "bug") in a sequence
- Identify and name animals

Pre-coding skill
- Debugging

Main language content

What animal is it? What color is it? It's (brown).
Animals: *cat, fish, leopard, monkey, polar bear, rabbit, whale*
Colors: *blue, brown, green, pink, red, white, yellow*

OPENING

Circle time

Materials and preparation
- Puppet
- Visual schedule pictures (hide them around the classroom)

Show the puppet to students and have them greet it with *hello* or *hi*. Remind students of the attention-getter and practice it with them:
T: *Let's take this road!*
S: *It's time to code!*
or
T: *Turn on your fun mode because it's time to…*
S: *Code!*
Hide the visual schedule pictures that refer to today's activities. Tell students to look for them around the classroom. As they find a picture, tell them to hand it to you. Then talk to students about each of the moments of the class.

> **Note to teachers**
> Remind students that they should be quiet and pay attention when you use the attention-getter.

Sing the *Animals song*.

Materials and preparation
- Audio library – songs

Sing the *Animals song* (track 16). Ask students to stand up, sing along, and do the actions.

ACTIVE LEARNING

Animal acting

Ask students to stand up. Call out the name of an animal from the *Animals song* (track 17) (*leopard, polar bear, monkey, whale*) or pets that students know (e.g. *dog, cat*). Students walk around the room pretending to be that animal.

Look and cross out.

Materials and preparation

- Project Book page 27

Help students open their Project Book to page 27. Point to the animals and ask them what they can see. Look at the first sequence. Point to each picture and ask, *What color is it?* Repeat with all of the pictures until you get to the picture that is different. After students identify the difference, say, *Uh-oh! It's a bug!* Ask them to draw an X to cross out the "bug". Repeat the procedure for the other sequences. Ask students what the "bugs" are (the wrong colors (cat and rabbit) and the wrong size (fish)).

> **Note to teachers**
> In coding, a "bug" is a mistake that prevents something from functioning correctly. This activity helps students associate this via pictures; they notice that the incorrect picture spoils the sequence.

DIFFERENTIATED INSTRUCTION

BELOW LEVEL
Look and cross out.

Give students plenty of help with identifying the "bug". Explore each picture with them until they find which one is different. Help them draw the X.

ABOVE LEVEL
Look and cross out.

Students can identify the "bug" and cross it out independently.

CLOSING

Fix the bug. Sing the *Goodbye song*.

Materials and preparation

- Audio library – songs
- Pictures of animals (at least two different animals; one picture per student)

Divide students into small groups. Ask one group to come to the front and turn away from the other group. Put the pictures of the animals face down. Ask each student to pick up a picture, but do not let students see which animal it is. They choose without seeing the "bug". Organize the students into a line, and then have them show the pictures they choose to the rest of the class. The other students have to identify the student with a different animal ("the bug"). A volunteer student can come up and lead the "bug" student away, in order to "fix" the problem.
Sing the *Goodbye song* (track 05) and invite students to sing along. Say *goodbye* to them and have them say *goodbye* back to you.

Unit 7 What is your favorite food?

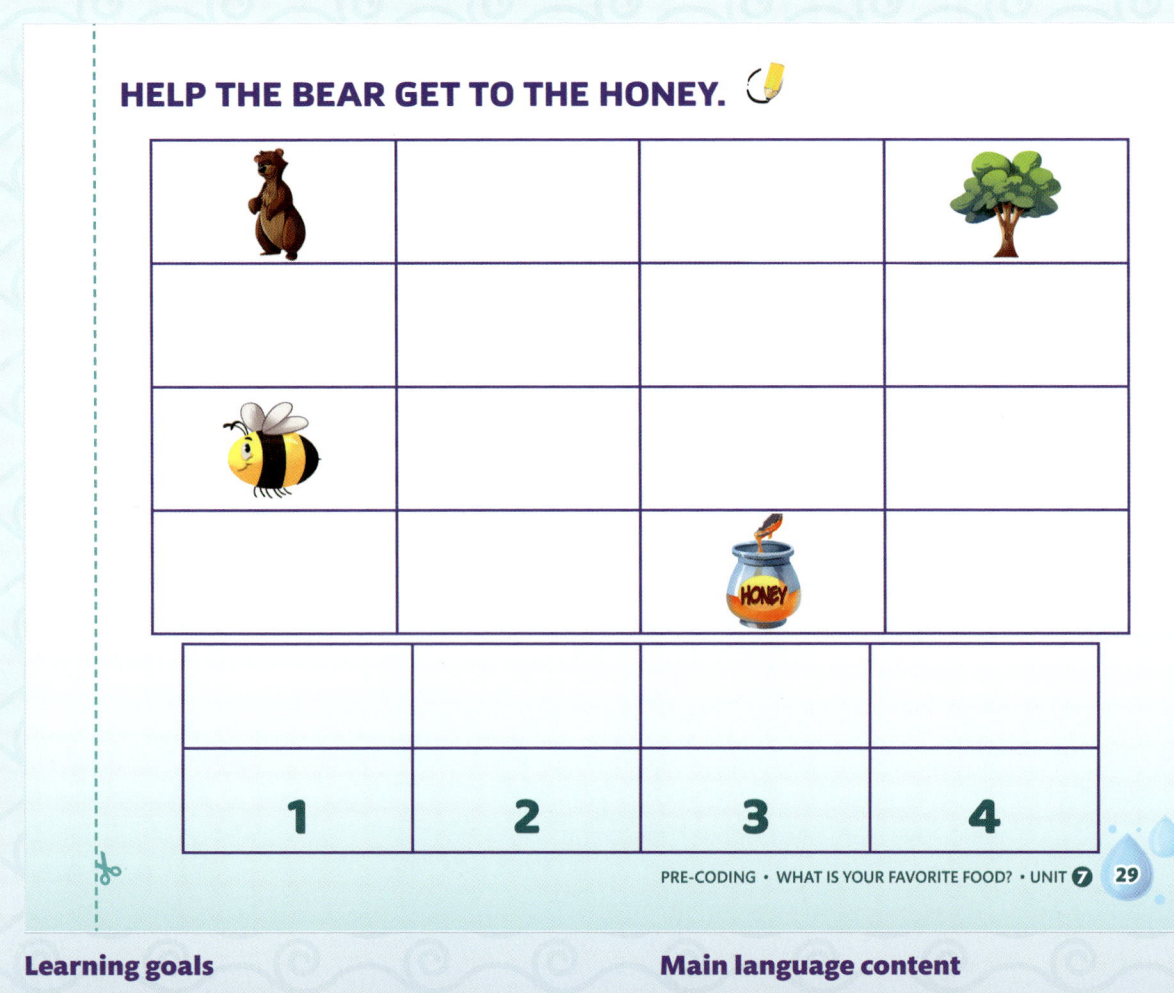

Learning goals
- Make an algorithm
- Practice using words for food

Pre-coding skill
- Sequence

Main language content
Colors: *blue, green, red, yellow*
Commands: *forward, right, stop*
Nature: *bear, bee, honey, tree*

OPENING

Circle time

Materials and preparation
- Audio library – songs
- Puppet
- Visual schedule pictures

Show the puppet to students and have them greet it with *hello* or *hi*. Sing the *Hello song* (track 04) and have them sing, mime, and dance. Remind students of the attention-getter and practice it with them:
T: *Let's take this road!*
S: *It's time to code!*
or
T: *Turn on your fun mode because it's time to…*
S: *Code!*
Have students sit in a circle. Show them the visual schedule pictures. Ask for volunteers to help you turn them over. Encourage the whole class to say what each picture shows. Choose a class helper of the day and have them order the pictures of the activities as they are mentioned.

> **Note to teachers**
> You can also teach/review the attention-getter *All set? You bet!*

Move forward, move right!
Say *forward* and take a step forward, then say *right* and take a step to the right. Continue chanting *forward, right* and taking the steps. Then invite students to stand up and join in. Shout *stop* at any given moment. Students have to sit down quickly on the floor. Repeat this a couple of times until students understand the words.

32 Pre-coding

ACTIVE LEARNING

Help the bear get to the honey.

Materials and preparation
- Aprons (if available)
- Crayons or pencils (optional)
- Paint (two different colors)
- Project Book page 29
- Sponge cut into thick arrow shapes (across → and down arrows ↓ – make sure these are the same size as the squares in the Project Book)
- Trays/Paper plates for paint

Help students open their Project Book to page 29. Point to the picture and ask students if they know what to do. Explain that they need to help the bear get to the honey.

Divide students into small groups or pairs. Give each group/pair two trays/plates of paint (two different colors) and arrow shapes. Help students choose a path to the honey, using the arrows. They print the arrows onto the page by pressing the arrows into the paint. They should press it twice: once into the main grid and once into the grid below to create the "code".

Alternatively, students can draw horizontal and vertical lines representing the across and down arrows. You can choose a color for vertical lines and another color for horizontal lines. Help students draw the lines as necessary.

> **Note to teachers**
> The grid below the main grid shows the instructions, or the "algorithm", for the bear to reach the honey.

DIFFERENTIATED INSTRUCTION

BELOW LEVEL
Help the bear get to the honey.

Students will need extra help pressing the shapes into the paint and then on the page.

ABOVE LEVEL
Help the bear get to the honey.

Students can work more independently. Ask them which arrows they have to use in each square and let them print them on the page.

CLOSING

Follow the instructions.
Sing the *Goodbye song*.

Materials and preparation
- Audio library – songs
- Set up a simple path in the classroom between the students and the board, placing a few "obstacles" (e.g. toys) in the way

Invite a volunteer student to stand up. Tell the other students that they need to help the student reach the board, but they need to avoid the obstacles. Remind students of *forward* and *right*. Students call out the instructions to help their classmate reach the board. You should set up expectations of walking safely so as to avoid accidents. Sing the *Goodbye song* (track 05) and invite students to sing along. Say *goodbye* to them and have them say *goodbye* back to you.

LOOK, COLOR, AND DRAW. 👁️ ✏️ 👄

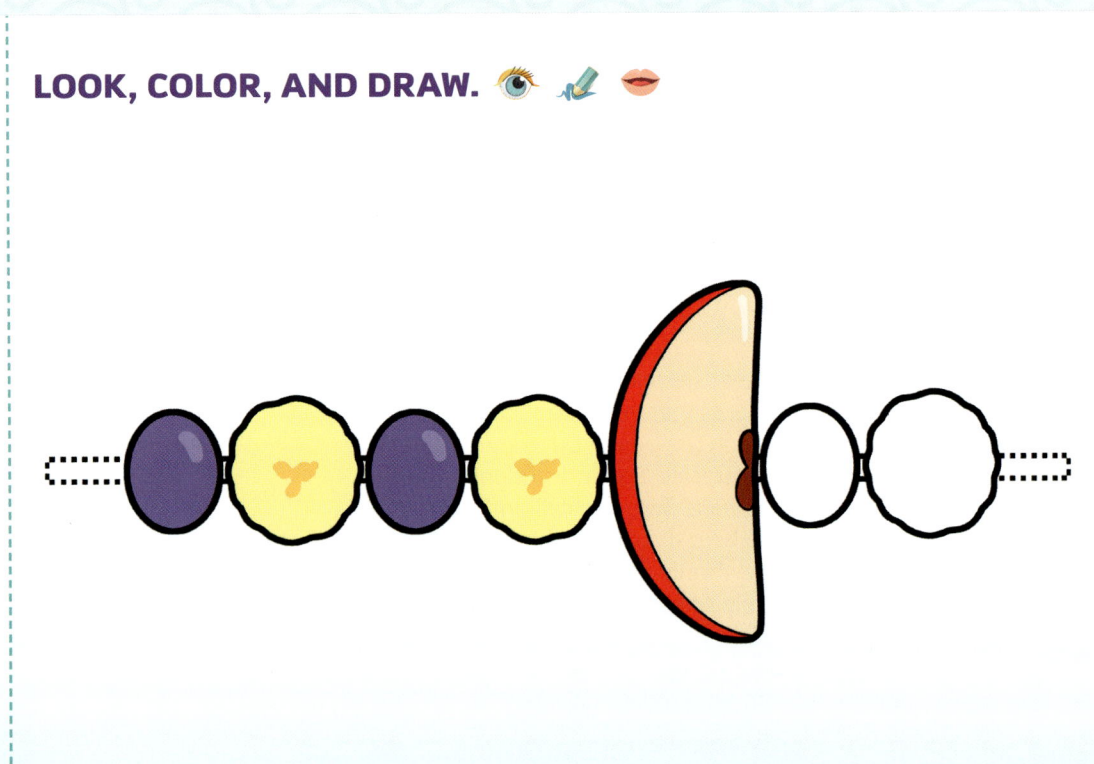

PRE-CODING • WHAT IS YOUR FAVORITE FOOD? • UNIT 7 • 31

Learning goals
- Identify and follow a sequence
- Identify and name fruits

Pre-coding skill
- Sequence

Main language content
What fruit is it? It's (a banana). What comes next?
Colors: *green, red, yellow*
Fruits: *apple, banana, grape*

OPENING

Circle time

Materials and preparation
- Puppet
- Visual schedule pictures

Show the puppet to students and have them greet it with *hello* or *hi*. Remind students of the attention-getter and practice it with them:
T: *Let's take this road!*
S: *It's time to code!*
or
T: *Turn on your fun mode because it's time to...*
S: *Code!*
Show students the visual schedule pictures. Ask for volunteers to help you turn them over. Encourage the whole class to say what each picture shows. Ask students to help you select the pictures that show today's schedule as you tell them what they are going to do today.

> **Note to teachers**
> Remind students that they should be quiet and pay attention when you use the attention-getter.

Fruit mystery bag

Materials and preparation
- A bag
- A selection of apples, bananas, and grapes (real or plastic)

Put the fruits in the bag. Ask students to sit in a circle. Show the mystery bag, ask, *What's inside?* and encourage students to share their ideas. Walk around the circle inviting students to put their hands in, feel the fruit inside, guess what it is, and then take it out. Help students name the fruit and say what color it is.

Pre-coding

ACTIVE LEARNING

Look, color, and draw.

Materials and preparation
- Crayons: purple and yellow
- Pencils
- Project Book page 31

Help students open their Project Book to page 31. Point at the fruit and ask, *What fruit is it?* Encourage students to identify the fruits. Say, *Yummy, it's a fruit kebab!* and rub your stomach. Explain that students are going to color the fruit kebab themselves. Point to each fruit and ask, *What fruit is it?* Ask, *What color is it?* and have students color the fruits to complete the pattern. Then they trace the kebab stick with their pencils and color it. When they finish, have them observe the sequence of fruits.

> **Note to teachers**
> When students have finished, you can use the bag of fruits from the previous activity for further practice. Volunteer students can take the fruit from the bag as you point to it on the page.

DIFFERENTIATED INSTRUCTION

BELOW LEVEL
Look, color, and draw.

Give students plenty of help with identifying the fruits and the color they have to use for each fruit.

ABOVE LEVEL
Look, color, and draw.

Students can draw the next fruit in the sequence.

CLOSING

Play *Fruit salad*. Sing the *Goodbye song*.

Materials and preparation
- A ball
- Audio library – songs
- Flashcards: *green*, *red*, *yellow* (several large copies)
- Large pictures of apples, bananas, and individual grapes (optional)

Tell students that they are going to play a game. Assign each student a fruit — apple, banana, or grape. Stick a printout of the fruit or the corresponding color to the students' T-shirts. Have students sit in a circle. Play a song from the audio library or a song that students like. Students pass a ball around the circle. When you stop the music, tap four students on the shoulder and call out their fruits in a specific order, e.g. *banana, grape, banana, grape*. These students rush to stand up and get in that order. Call out the order again and encourage the other students to say if the sequence is correct. Repeat the activity for as long as you there is time left in the class. You should set up expectations of walking safely so as to avoid accidents.
Sing the *Goodbye song* (track 05) and invite students to sing along. Say *goodbye* to them and have them say *goodbye* back to you.

Unit 8 What do you like about school?

STICK. TELL YOUR CLASSMATE.

PRE-CODING • WHAT DO YOU LIKE ABOUT SCHOOL? • UNIT 8   33

Learning goals
- Make an algorithm
- Ask and answer about locations

Pre-coding skill
- Programming

Main language content
Pass it to (Daniel).
Prepositions: *on, under*
School objects: *book, chair, pencil, table*

OPENING

Circle time

Materials and preparation
- Audio library – songs
- Puppet
- Visual schedule pictures

Show the puppet to students and have them greet it with *hello* or *hi*. Sing the *Hello song* (track 04) and have them sing, mime, and dance. Remind students of the attention-getter and practice it with them:
T: *Let's take this road!*
S: *It's time to code!*
or
T: *Turn on your fun mode because it's time to…*
S: *Code!*
Have students sit in a circle. Show them the visual schedule pictures. Ask for volunteers to help you turn them over. Encourage the whole class to say what each picture shows. Choose a class helper of the day and have them order the pictures of the activities as they are mentioned.

> **Note to teachers**
> You can also teach/review the attention-getter *All set? You bet!*

Sing the *School song*.

Materials and preparation
- Audio library – songs
- Books (one per pair of students)
- Pencils (one per pair of students)

Play the *School song* (track 19). Ask students to stand up, join in with the singing, and do the actions. Show the pencil and the book, say the words, and have students repeat after you. Give each pair of students a pencil and a book. Play the song again, and encourage students to dance in their pairs. Pause the audio and say *pencil* or *book*. Students show the correct object.

Pre-coding

> **Note for teacher**
> Working in pairs at this age means that students can support each other.

ACTIVE LEARNING

Play *Pass the ball*.

Materials and preparation

- A ball

Have students stand up and make a circle. Take a ball and pass it around the circle. Then take the ball back, say, *Pass it to (Daniel)* and give it to that student. Then say, *Pass it to (another student's name.)* The student passes it to that student. Continue this way until all students have passed the ball.

Put an individual desk in the middle of the circle. Place the ball on the table and say *on*. Then put it under the table and say *under*. Repeat this several times, encouraging students to join in with you as you say the words. Then invite students to come into the middle of the circle, give them an instruction, and they put the ball in the correct place.

> **Note for teacher**
> At this age, students learn by copying, so make sure you give plenty of demonstration and choose more confident students to go first.

Stick. Tell your classmate.

Materials and preparation

- A book
- A pencil
- Project Book page 33

Show a pencil and exaggeratedly act out putting it on your desk/a table all students can see. Help students say *on*. Repeat with *book* and *under*.

Help students open their Project Book to page 33. Point to the picture and help them notice it shows a table and a chair. Then help students turn to the stickers page at the back of the book and identify the stickers for Unit 8. Have them peel off the first book and pencil stickers. They stick them *on* or *under* the desk in the first picture. Help them with the stickers as needed.

Then they get the second book and pencil stickers. In pairs, they tell each other where to stick them using *on* or *under*.

> **Note to teachers**
> Encourage students to say *on* or *under* as they work together. However, at this age, they will probably show each other by pointing. Praise them for working well together.

DIFFERENTIATED INSTRUCTION

BELOW LEVEL
Stick. Tell your classmate.

Students may not be able to work in pairs, so you could support them to work in small groups or adapt the activity to a whole-class one, with you giving the instructions for them to stick the second stickers.

ABOVE LEVEL
Stick. Tell your classmate.

Materials and preparation

- Crayons or colored pencils

Students can draw other school objects in the pictures and say if they are *on* or *under* the table/chair.

CLOSING

Follow the instructions. Sing the *Goodbye song*.

Materials and preparation

- Audio library – songs
- Crayons
- Sheets of paper (one per student)

Tell students that they are going to be "computers" and you are going to be a "coder". Give each student a sheet of paper and some crayons. Give them an instruction, e.g. *Draw a dog*. Students draw until you say *stop*. When you say *stop*, they put their crayons down. Then say *show* and they show their pictures to their classmates. Praise students for following your instructions.

Sing the *Goodbye song* (track 05) and invite students to sing along. Say *goodbye* to them and have them say *goodbye* back to you.

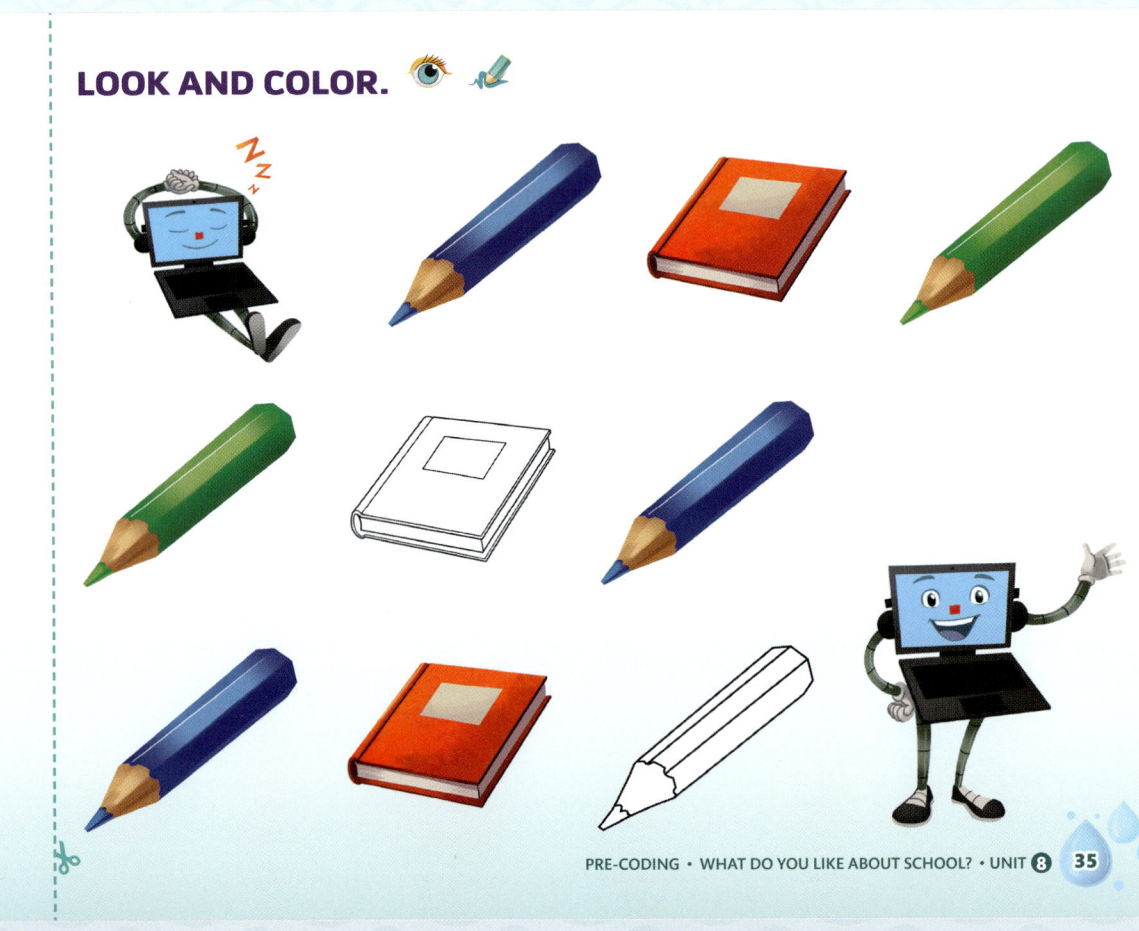

Learning goals
- Identify and complete a pattern
- Identify and use words for classroom objects

Pre-coding skill
- Pattern

Main language content
What color is it? It's (blue). What comes next?
Classroom objects: *book, pencil*
Colors: *green, red, yellow*

OPENING

Circle time

Materials and preparation
- Puppet
- Visual schedule pictures (hide them around the classroom)

Show the puppet to students and have them greet it with *hello* or *hi*. Remind students of the attention-getter and practice it with them:
T: *Let's take this road!*
S: *It's time to code!*
or
T: *Turn on your fun mode because it's time to…*
S: *Code!*
Hide the visual schedule pictures that refer to today's activities. Tell students to look for them around the classroom. As they find a picture, tell them to hand it to you. Then talk to students about each of the moments of the class.

> **Note to teachers**
> Remind students that they should be quiet and pay attention when you use the attention-getter.

Sing *School supplies.*

Materials and preparation
- Audio library – songs

Ask students to stand up. Sing *School supplies* (track 12). Invite students to stand up, sing, and do the actions.

ACTIVE LEARNING

Book and pencil

Materials and preparation

- Several books and pencils, hidden around the classroom

Say to students, *Oh, no. I lost my book. I lost my pencil*. Ask them to help you find them. Invite a few students to walk around the classroom, looking for the hidden items. Make sure you hide the objects in an obvious place, so that the other students can help by calling out *hot* and *cold* as the students looking get closer. You should set up expectations of walking safely so as to avoid accidents.
Once they have collected in all of the pencils and books ask them to sit in a circle. And place some of the items in a pattern, e.g. book, pencil, book, pencil, in the middle of the circle. Invite volunteer students to complete the pattern with alternating books and pencils.

Look and color.

Materials and preparation

- Crayons: blue, green, and red
- Flashcards: *blue, green, red*
- Project Book page 35

Help students open their Project Book to page 35. Hand out the crayons. Hold up the flashcards one by one, and ask students to hold up the corresponding crayon. Point to the pictures in the book and ask students, *What color is it?* When you get to the blank image, encourage students to say what color it should be and help them notice the pattern. Students color the blank images in the correct color (red book, green pencil).

DIFFERENTIATED INSTRUCTION

BELOW LEVEL
Sing *School supplies*.

Praise students for joining in with the actions/dancing, even if they are confident enough to sing.

ABOVE LEVEL
Look and color.

Materials and preparation

- Crayons or colored pencils
- Sheets of paper

Students can draw and color the next picture in the sequence on a separate sheet of paper.

CLOSING

Role-play being computers and coders. Sing the *Goodbye song*.

Materials and preparation

- Audio library – songs

Tell students that they have done various activities and have acted as "coders" and "computers". Remind them that the coders tell the computer to do something. Explain that you are the computer, and they are the coder so they can tell you to do anything! As they give you instructions, encourage them to use words they have learned this year. Sing the *Goodbye song* (track 05) and invite students to sing along. Say *goodbye* to them and have them say *goodbye* back to you. Congratulate students on completing all of the projects in their Pre-coding Project Book.

Notes

Notes

Notes

Notes

Notes

Notes

Notes

Notes

Notes